INDUSTRIAL CONCENTRATION AND INFLATION

Steven Lustgarten
with a foreword by Yale Brozen

American Enterprise Institute for Public Policy Research
Washington, D.C.

Steven Lustgarten is associate professor of economics and finance at Baruch College, City University of New York.

HG
538
L87

ISBN 0-8447-3169-2

Domestic Affairs Study 31, June 1975

Library of Congress Catalog Card No. 75-18501

Printed in the United States of America

CONTENTS

FOREWORD

It is frequently argued that industries in which a few firms produce most of the output charge higher prices than they would if the large, component firms were broken into several smaller ones (as was done, for example, with the old Standard Oil Company and the American Tobacco Company early in the century). Whether or not the argument is valid, and much evidence to the contrary has appeared, it does not follow that inflation is a consequence of a highly concentrated industrial structure. Assuming, for the sake of argument, that concentrated industries charge higher prices, we should suffer *rising* prices only if industrial concentration were rising. But data for the U.S. economy show average market concentration levels to be fairly stable. That being the case, no connection should be expected between industrial concentration and inflation.

Professor Lustgarten examines the movement of prices of manufacturing industries. He seeks to determine whether prices in the more concentrated industries increase more rapidly than those in the less concentrated industries. He finds that the price behavior of the highly concentrated industries has not been a source of inflation in the United States. According to his data, the prices of these defamed industries have not only *not* been a source of inflation, but have risen more slowly than those in atomistic industries. They have, in fact, been a moderating factor in inflation.

This superb performance on the part of our concentrated industries should not come as a surprise. In the last few years we have observed prices rising in our most highly atomistic industries — those in agriculture — at a far more rapid pace than in any other sector of the economy. The lesson should be clear that atomizing an industry is not the way to cure an existing inflation or prevent future inflations.

1

This lesson was learned by the English and the Japanese some time ago. Instead of breaking up firms in their concentrated industries, their policy has favored and subsidized consolidation. Mergers have been encouraged instead of condemned. In practice this may be as unwarranted a policy as deconcentration, since economies of scale are not available in every industry. Some industries are more efficient and progressive if concentrated, some if not so concentrated. There are no magic formulas equally applicable to all industries and all circumstances.

Yet Professor Lustgarten's data demonstrate that output per man-hour has increased more rapidly in our more concentrated than in our less concentrated industries. This may be a consequence of economies of scale realized through growth — that is, economies that are available to a concentrated industry (the reason the industry is concentrated) but not available to an atomistic industry (again, the reason it is not concentrated). The more rapid rise in productivity in concentrated industries has meant a relative drop in "unit labor costs and lower prices," according to Professor Lustgarten. "The fact that larger increases in productivity in concentrated industries have been translated into lower prices is evidence that these industries are competitive. . . . The behavior of productivity suggests that deconcentration is likely to produce higher rather than lower prices."

Yale Brozen

Graduate School of Business
University of Chicago

INDUSTRIAL CONCENTRATION
AND INFLATION

1. Introduction and Summary

The hypothesis that continuous price inflation is a direct consequence of market power possessed by firms in concentrated industries has generated considerable controversy in recent years. It has been a topic of heated debate in economic literature,[1] prompted an extended series of congressional hearings,[2] provided a strong rationale for the institution of wage-price controls, and formed the basis for a proposed Industrial Reorganization Act.[3] This study examines some of the theoretical arguments used to relate industrial concentration to the problem of inflation. It also presents empirical evidence on the behavior of prices, wages, and productivity in concentrated and nonconcentrated industries and reaches the conclusion, based on the evidence, that inflation is not related to industrial concentration.

The author expresses thanks to Professor J. Fred Weston for the inspiration and encouragement that led to research in the area of industrial concentration, to Professor Yale Brozen for reviewing initial drafts of this paper and contributing important ideas, to Mary Wilkinson for research assistance, and to Jane Harrison and Helen Cavanna for help in typing the manuscript.

[1] A summary of the literature can be found in Frederic M. Scherer, *Industrial Market Structure and Economic Performance* (Chicago: Rand McNally & Co., 1970), pp. 284–303; see also, "Concentration, Inflation and Unemployment," *Concentration, Competition and Efficiency* (Washington, D.C.: Chamber of Commerce of the United States, 1974), pp. 18–21.

[2] U.S. Congress, Senate, Subcommittee on Antitrust and Monopoly of the Committee on the Judiciary, *Hearings on Administered Prices*, 85th Congress, 2d session, 1958, part 1.

[3] The statement by Senator Philip Hart in introducing this bill to Congress indicates that reduction of inflation and unemployment is the objective of his proposed legislation (S.1167). See U.S. Congress, "Statements on Introduced Bills and Joint Resolutions," *Congressional Record*, July 24, 1972, p. S11495.

Despite the lack of evidence linking industrial concentration to the rising price level, powerful proponents of this view have urged structural reform of industry — deconcentration — as a means for mitigating inflation. A cabinet committee study under President Lyndon B. Johnson recommended such action. Senator Philip Hart, in his speech introducing his industrial reorganization bill, argued that inflation would be slowed by breaking up large corporations in industries where four or fewer firms produced more than 50 percent of the output. The Federal Trade Commission (FTC) answered congressional requests to do something to reduce gasoline and fuel oil prices by filing a complaint demanding the dissolution of the eight largest petroleum refining companies, despite the fact that these companies ranked only in the mid-range of concentration among American manufacturing industries.

Arguments of the Cabinet Committee Study. President Johnson, in 1968, established the Cabinet Committee on Price Stability to "develop a long term program complementing monetary and fiscal policy by attacking structural sources of inflation."[4] The committee's second study paper entitled "Industrial Structure and Competition Policy" appeared in January 1969, at a time when the inflationary pressures built up by deficit spending and monetary expansion were reaching a peak. The stated goal of the study was to discuss "both the ways in which business enterprises with discretionary market power may exert inflationary pressures and recent empirical findings that demonstrate a critical link between market power of both labor and business and the inflation problem."

Despite its objective, most of the material had little relevance to inflation. Of the study's more than fifty pages, only four were devoted to the role of market structure in promoting inflation. The rest covered aggregate concentration trends, levels and trends in market concentration, the role of mergers in promoting concentration, and policies for fostering competition. Although the staff study stated that market structure is related to inflation, its evidence dealt only with the existing industry structure and recent changes in it. Nowhere did it present any systematic evidence relating the rate of price change to the level of industry concentration or to changes in the level of concentration.

---

[4] Cabinet Committee on Price Stability, "Study Paper Number 2: Industrial Structure and Competition Policy," *Studies by the Staff of the Cabinet Committee on Price Stability* (Washington, D.C.: U.S. Government Printing Office, January 1969).

Proof by selected example. The only direct evidence presented was a few statistics on the steel industry for the years 1953-59. These statistics purported to show that prices rose despite the existence of excess capacity. No other industry was mentioned and, despite readily available data, no other time period was discussed. One might ask if steel was the only concentrated industry and if the period 1953-59 was the only one in which its price rise was higher than average.

If the game of proof by selected example is to be played, we could select the examples of household refrigerators (SIC# 3632) and household laundry equipment (SIC# 3633). These industries are even more concentrated than steel. Their experience "proves" that the more concentrated our industries, the less inflation we have.[5] Prices in these industries were virtually unchanged or declined between 1960 and 1972, while the wholesale price index (WPI) for all items rose by 25 percent.[6] If we believe that selected examples are sufficient foundation for the adoption of a policy, these examples "prove" we should enact an industrial reorganization bill *to force mergers* among small firms in order to mitigate inflation.

Theoretical arguments. The authors of the cabinet committee study mentioned several ways in which they supposed industrial concentration promotes inflation. The first was by allowing firms "to exact persistently high profits." However, the relation of high profits to the inflationary process is of dubious significance. If profits actually were "persistently high" in concentrated industries (the issue is as yet unresolved),[7] it would mean that prices were too high in these industries but too low in other industries. Inflation occurs when the overall price level (average of prices in all industries) rises.

---

[5] These industries were cited by the cabinet committee study as examples of large and highly concentrated industries. Household refrigerators (SIC# 3632) and household laundry equipment (SIC# 3633) have four-firm concentration ratios of 72 percent and 79 percent respectively. The steel industry products which were cited by the committee are all part of SIC# 3312, which has a four-firm concentration ratio of only 50 percent. The five-digit product categories within steel cited by the cabinet committee study range in concentration from 61 to 70 percent. Ibid., p. 93.

[6] A compilation from industry trade journals showed that in 1960 the average price of a refrigerator was $325 and in 1972 it was only $344. This represents an increase of less than 6 percent. For a clothes washer in the same period, the average price fell from $252 to $245, a decline of 2.8 percent. See Guenther Baumgart, "Industry Still Provides Bargains," *NAM Reports*, vol. 19 (January 21, 1974), p. 6.

[7] Harold Demsetz, *The Market Concentration Doctrine* (Washington, D.C.: American Enterprise Institute, 1973); Yale Brozen, "The Persistence of High Rates of Return in High-Stable Concentration Industries," *Journal of Law & Economics*, vol. 19 (October 1971), pp. 501–12.

Thus, continuously rising profits might be inflationary,[8] but continuously high profits have no relevance to inflation.

If concentration were increasing in major industries, and if increased concentration produces higher prices with no offsetting declines in other industries, the result might be inflationary. However, the staff study itself acknowledged that "average market concentration in manufacturing industries has shown no marked tendency to increase or decrease between 1947 and 1966. . . ."[9]

A second argument of the staff study was that industrial concentration contributes to inflation because it allows sellers "to pass through significant increases in costs." Presumably, cost increases incurred by only one firm in an atomistic market are not likely to be followed by a price increase since it would result in a substantial loss of sales. On the other hand, when cost increases such as industry-wide union wage increases or rising material prices are incurred by all firms simultaneously, the ability of firms to raise prices is unlikely to be affected by the number of sellers in the industry. Whether the firm is atomistic or oligopolistic, a compensating price increase which is not matched by rival firms will significantly reduce the sales of that firm.[10]

The cabinet committee study provides further elaboration on the influence of industrial concentration on the "wage-price spiral." It states that "large profits may serve as an enticing target" for union wage demands.[11] It refers to several studies which show that wage increases are generally related to the level of profits and to increases in profits. However, this positive relationship between profitability and wages is not unique to concentrated industries. Rising profits generally reflect increases in demand for industrial output. Increased demand can be expected to produce an increase in demand for labor, which in turn raises wages. In this case, price increases are generated more directly by rising demand than by rising profits.

It is possible that persistently high profits earned by an industry, as a result of a monopoly position, might cause labor to try to

---

[8] Assuming that the rising profits come from rising prices and not from decreasing costs.

[9] Cabinet Committee on Price Stability, "Study Paper Number 2," p. 58.

[10] The term "atomistic" refers to a market composed of many sellers, each of which is too small to have a significant influence on the market price and output. This type is contrasted with an oligopolistic market, which is comprised of several large and interdependent sellers. In the case of oligopoly, the price charged by one seller can have a significant influence on the quantity sold by other sellers and, in setting price, the oligopolist takes into account the expected reaction from other sellers.

[11] Cabinet Committee on Price Stability, "Study Paper Number 2," p. 41.

capture a share of the profits through higher wages. But this would imply a relation between industrial concentration and excess profits which is still the subject of considerable debate. Although some studies have observed such a relation, the profits could also be the result of managerial efficiencies, economies of scale, temporary excess demand, or poor data.[12]

The cabinet committee study merely asserts that "firms with considerable discretion over wage and price decisions may cause inflationary pressures even in the absence of full employment."[13] It never demonstrates that wage and price decisions of such firms play any more than a *de minimus* role in inflation or that these firms even have "discretion over wage and price decisions."

Industrial Reorganization. The latest application of the concentration-inflation hypothesis is the legislation proposed by Senator Philip Hart, entitled the Industrial Reorganization Act. Its objective is to deconcentrate many of the major manufacturing industries. Economic justification for this legislation was given by Hart in his introductory statement: "These industries were selected because based on our research and all available to us we determined that they have the greatest impact on the persistent inflation eating away at the Nation.[14] The evidence or research referred to by Senator Hart is not set forth in the proposal.

Before undertaking a program which will involve restructuring large segments of the economy, there should be evidence that substantial benefits will accrue. So far, this evidence has not been produced. The evidence presented below implies, on the contrary, that deconcentration would have no moderating impact on inflation.

Summary of Findings. Section 2 continues the discussion of theoretical arguments which have been used to link industrial concentration with inflation. Despite their initial appeal, a careful analysis of the evidence reveals that these arguments have little support. Section 3 reviews earlier economic studies which appear to support the position that industrial concentration promotes inflation. The statistical results of these studies are shown to be ambiguous in that they can be used to support a full range of effects — inflation, defla-

---

[12] Stanley I. Ornstein, "Concentration and Profits," *Journal of Business*, vol. 45 (October 1972), pp. 519–41, finds no relation between profitability and industrial concentration. Yale Brozen, "Concentration and Profits: Does Concentration Matter?" *Antitrust Bulletin*, vol. 19 (Summer 1974), pp. 381–99, also found no relationship.
[13] Cabinet Committee on Price Stability, "Study Paper Number 2," p. 39.
[14] See the statement by Senator Philip Hart cited in footnote 3.

tion, or no effect. The authors, using similar data and statistical methods, observe opposite effects of concentration in the same time periods, and yet view their results as supporting the same theory.

Section 4 presents evidence on price and cost behavior in concentrated and unconcentrated industries. It shows that, over the long run, prices in highly concentrated industries have risen more slowly than other prices. The principal reason has been greater increases in productivity (output per man-hour) in concentrated industries. This has led to lower unit labor costs and lower prices. The fact that larger increases in productivity in concentrated industries have been translated into lower prices is evidence that these industries are competitive (see Figure 1). The behavior of productivity suggests that deconcentration is likely to produce higher rather than lower prices.

2. The Theory of Market Power Inflation

Inflation has traditionally been viewed as a phenomenon which arises when buyers try to purchase more goods and services at the existing price level than the economy has the capacity to produce. Prices rise as the existing resources are bid away from competing alternatives. They continue to rise as long as aggregate demand rises more rapidly than aggregate supply.

The traditional view is that excessive aggregate demand is caused by government deficit spending and monetary expansion. In recent years, however, some authors have begun to argue that it is not buyers but sellers or their suppliers who cause inflation. They make a distinction between the traditional type of inflation, labeled "demand-pull," and other types of inflation, characterized as "administered inflation" and as "cost-push." The newer theory holds that inflation occurs when sellers raise prices in order to raise their profits or unions force wage increases to raise their share of the national income. In the latter case, prices rise because employers must cover their higher costs.

Discretionary Power. The traditional view is that administered or cost-push inflation is impossible in a competitive market because any seller raising his price would quickly find his sales and profits declining. But those who argue administered or cost-push inflation emphasize that the economy is imperfectly competitive and that such sellers as oligopolistic firms and labor unions have some discretion over what price to set. Their control has been labeled "discretionary power," "market power," or "administrative power." While prices

Figure 1

INDUSTRIAL CONCENTRATION AND PRICES

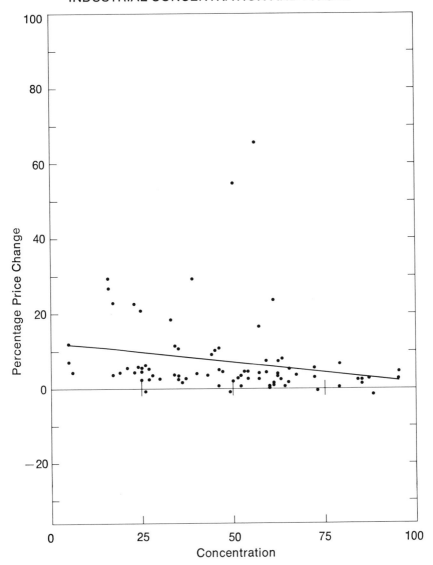

Note: Price change is the average annual percentage price change, 1971-73. Concentration is the four-firm concentration ratio in 1970.

Source: Price changes are taken from Appendix B. Concentration ratios are taken from Bureau of the Census, *Annual Survey of Manufactures, 1970: Value of Shipment Concentration Ratios* (Washington, D.C.: U.S. Government Printing Office, November 1972).

in atomistic industries are determined by the impersonal forces of supply and demand, oligopolistic prices are thought to be arbitrarily set at the sellers' discretion.

The dichotomy between discretionary and market prices is an over-simplification and, even if basically correct, is unrelated to inflation. Common observations reveal that many sellers that are not oligopolists have discretion over price. The average retail or service establishment is an example of a seller which, although one of many in a given area, would certainly not be classified as an oligopolist. Even the corner grocer has some discretion. Raising the price of a container of milk by a cent or two will not cause the amount of milk sold to fall to zero, although it may cause the amount to fall to unprofitable levels.[15] Almost every manufacturing, trade, or service company has the ability to charge alternative prices, at least in the very short run. The usual assumption is that sellers seek a price which yields maximum profits in the long run.

While all sellers have some discretionary power, the degree of discretion differs between industries. The "degree of discretion" depends on the effect of a change in price on the number of units sold. Thus, the degree of discretionary power is related to the elasticity or sensitivity of demand to changes in price.

Many believe that the quantity sold by an oligopolistic seller is less sensitive to price changes than that sold by an atomistic seller. The reason is thought to be that an increase in price by the atomistic seller will shift sales to rival sellers who then quickly expand their output to accommodate the new customers. However, the threat of rival firms exists in oligopoly also. If rivals are willing to expand output, the elasticity of demand facing the oligopolistic seller will be similar to that in an atomistic market. In picking the best of alternative prices, the oligopolistic firm as well as the atomistic firm has to consider the prices that rival firms are setting. The process of setting the best price is basically the same in the manufacture of steel as in retailing.

The only difference is the likelihood of collusion among existing sellers to set a higher price than might otherwise exist. A number of analysts believe that this likelihood is greater when sellers are fewer[16] and, therefore, greater in concentrated industries. But even if existing

---

[15] For examples, see M. A. Adelman, *A & P: A Study in Price-Cost Behavior and Public Policy* (Cambridge, Mass.: Harvard University Press, 1966).

[16] George J. Stigler demonstrated that when the number of sellers is lower, the ability to detect price cutters is much stronger and a collusive agreement easier to maintain. "A Theory of Oligopoly," *Journal of Political Economy*, vol. 72 (February 1964), pp. 44–61.

sellers are better able to set prices when they are few in number, their ability to maintain high prices and earn excessive profits is limited by potential new sellers and by the profitability of "cheating" on the agreement. Therefore, a small number of sellers does not guarantee high prices. However, as will be demonstrated below, even if discretionary power does lead to high price levels, it is still not relevant to inflation. Inflation is brought about not by prices which are "too high" but by prices which rise continually over time.

Irrelevance of Discretionary Power to Inflation. The relevance of discretionary power to inflation is thought to be the ability of sellers who possess it to raise price at any time, even though demand for output is unchanged. If sellers in many industries were simultaneously to raise price, and to do so again and again, the result would be a rising overall price level and an administered inflation.

In response to these propositions, one must ask whether there is not an optimal price beyond which further increases reduce profits as sales decline. The optimal price would thus be the price which, given current market conditions, including the likelihood of new entries and union activity, leads to the maximum long-run profits. For those who reject profit maximization as a realistic objective, the optimal price could be the price which earns enough profits to satisfy stockholders, discourages new entries in the markets, and allows managers "the easy life." Even if the optimal price is the result of oligopolistic collusion, once it is established, there is no reason to raise it unless market conditions change.[17]

If changing market conditions are the factor which causes prices to rise continually, then oligopolistic sellers are merely responding to rather than initiating inflationary forces. As long as the current price is optimal, further increases are self-defeating. To regard a particular period of inflation as the result of administered prices or a cost-push process requires the holder of such a belief to explain why sellers, who for some reason were not previously setting optimal prices, simultaneously decided to raise prices.

Those who believe that inflations are caused by oligopolists continually increasing prices or unions continually pushing up wage rates have never answered the question why oligopolists and unions stopped this activity from 1948 to 1950, when prices fell, in the late fifties, and in the first half of the sixties. And why did they resume

---

[17] As Professor James Tobin points out, "Monopolists have no reason to hold reserves of unexploited power." "Inflation and Unemployment," *American Economic Review*, vol. 62 (March 1972), p. 16.

their inflationary behavior in the early fifties and again in the mid-sixties?

Rigidity of Administered Prices. One theory relating monopoly power to inflation can be traced to the writings of Gardiner Means, who introduced the term "administered price" in describing noncompetitive price behavior. Initially, Means identified the failure of administered prices to decline as a major factor in causing depression.[18] In later years, however, Means considered administered prices to be an important cause of inflation.[19] Means never provided a precise method of identifying administered prices nor did he give an explanation of what caused these prices to behave as postulated. Both omissions have been major sources of confusion for those trying to test the administered-price thesis empirically. Initially, frequency of price change and, later, amplitude were used to identify administered prices. Over time, administered prices have become synonymous with oligopoly prices, despite the failure of writers such as DePodwin, Selden, and Phlips to find any association between rigidity or amplitude of price change and industry concentration.[20]

A basic characteristic attributed to administered prices is inflexibility, or insensitivity, to changes in demand (and sometimes to changes in cost). It is argued that oligopolists adjust to fluctuations in demand by altering their rate of output rather than their price. When price is altered, it is done only after a considerable lag. Gardiner Means set forth the relation between lagging administered prices and inflation by contrasting price behavior in the years 1942-53 with that in the years 1953-59:

> In the beginning of a demand inflation, market dominated prices tend to rise more rapidly while administrative-dominated prices lag well behind. Then in a period of readjustment, market dominated prices fall back while administrative-dominated prices continue to rise until the two

---

[18] Gardiner Means, *Industrial Prices and Their Relative Inflexibility*, a report to the secretary of agriculture published as S. Doc. No. 13, 74th Congress, 1st session, January 1935.

[19] Gardiner Means, "The Administered Price Thesis Reconfirmed," *American Economic Review*, vol. 67 (June 1972), pp. 292-306, and *Administrative Inflation and Public Policy* (Washington, D.C.: Anderson Kramer Associates, 1959).

[20] H. DePodwin and R. Selden, "Business Pricing Policies and Inflation," *Journal of Political Economy*, vol. 71 (April 1963), pp. 116–27; Louis Phlips, "Business Pricing Policies and Inflation — Some Evidence from EEC Countries," *Journal of Industrial Economics*, vol. 18 (November 1969), pp. 1–14.

groups are more nearly in balance. . . . Thus, administrative-dominated prices help to slow up the classical inflation rather than initiate it. Only in the later stages of this demand inflation did administered prices catch up with the general rise.[21]

While Means's thesis was essentially an empirical observation, a theoretical basis was later provided by Ackley, Galbraith, and Lerner.[22] It postulated that differences (between atomistic and oligopolistic industries) in the mechanism by which demand increases are translated into price increases result in a substantial response lag in the concentrated industries. Administered inflation can therefore be seen as a temporarily higher rate of price increase in concentrated industries as oligopolists catch up with prior shifts in demand. During this period, price may appear unresponsive to changes in current market conditions although it is actually responding to previous changes. This is the theoretical explanation of "counter-cyclical price behavior."

Sources of rigid prices. A common explanation for inflexible prices is that strongly interdependent firms may set prices above the competitive level. The ability to do so rests on the tacit (or sometimes overt) collusion of most firms in the industry. Any alteration of the status quo involves a risk of upsetting the collusive agreement. Furthermore, changes in industry demand are not always easily recognized. Any unilateral decrease in price may touch off a price war. Any unilateral increase may not be imitated. Thus, when market conditions change, oligopolists prefer to wait for some tacit industry consensus to form or for the industry price leader (if there is one) to initiate the appropriate change.

An alternative explanation of the apparent rigidity of industrial prices was offered by George J. Stigler and James K. Kindahl. They suggest, and demonstrate, that price rigidity is in part an illusion created by poor data. The price statistics reported by the Bureau of Labor Statistics (BLS) — where Means discovered administered

---

[21] Means, *Administrative Inflation and Public Policy*, p. 9.

[22] Garner Ackley, "Administered Prices and the Inflationary Process," *American Economic Review*, vol. 49 (May 1959), pp. 419–61; John K. Galbraith, "Market Structure and Stabilization Policy," *Review of Economics and Statistics*, vol. 39 (May 1957), pp. 124–33; Abba Lerner, "Sellers Inflation and Administered Depression," *Administered Prices: A Compendium on Public Policy*, prepared for the Senate Judiciary Committee, 88th Congress, 1st session (Washington, D.C.: U.S. Government Printing Office, 1963), pp. 196–212.

(rigid) prices — generally reflect "quoted" or "list" prices rather than actual (transactions) prices.[23]

Economists have always suspected that the nominally rigid quoted prices did not represent at all accurately the actual behavior of the prices at which important transactions take place. Two recent studies now offer persuasive support for the suspicion.

The first study, by McAllister, makes comparisons of wholesale price quotations from January, 1957, through December, 1959, with prices paid by large private buyers. In each case the buying price is that of a single company and is therefore more rigid than it would be if several buyers were represented.

A total of 30 comparisons is reported. In only two cases (waste paper and mercury) did the BLS quotations change more frequently, and both were cases where the BLS price was not rigid. In the group as a whole, company prices changed 236 times compared with 127 changes in BLS prices, so even single-buyer quotations were almost twice as flexible. . . . The general conclusion is clear: the BLS greatly underestimated the frequency of price changes, and — it may be added — the amplitude of price changes.

The second study, by John Flueck, utilizes the bids on government purchase contracts. . . . The government bid prices show a change whenever two successive contracts are compared: there were 310 out of 319 possible price changes. The BLS price quotations, on the other hand, showed only 191 changes. Flueck also shows that the amplitude of price fluctuations is on the order of three times as large as the BLS reports.[24]

In a more recent study, Stigler and Kindahl obtained actual transactions prices from the buyers of industrial products. They found these to be significantly more variable than the BLS prices. The differences were greatest in periods when transactions prices were falling. In two business contractions occurring during their period of study, there were almost twice as many instances of price decreases

---

[23] For further evidence on the limitations of price statistics reported by the Bureau of Labor Statistics, see Harry E. McAllister, *Government Price Statistics*, Staff Paper No. 8 of the Joint Economic Committee (Washington, D.C.: U.S. Government Printing Office, January 21, 1961); George J. Stigler, "Administered Prices and Oligopolistic Inflation," *Journal of Business of the University of Chicago*, vol. 35 (January 1962), reprinted in Stigler, *The Organization of Industry* (Homewood, Ill.: Richard D. Irwin, 1968).

[24] Stigler, *The Organization of Industry*, pp. 241–43.

in actual (transactions) prices as in BLS prices.[25] Stigler and Kindahl also observed that during the latter half of their study period, 1961-66, the BLS trend of price increases was 0.7 percent a year faster than the trend of transactions prices.

Cost plus pricing and demand inflexibility. Another common explanation for rigid prices is that in oligopoly prices are set at the sellers' discretion according to some rule or judgment whereas in atomistic industry prices are determined by impersonal market forces. Thus, while the response of market prices is considered "automatic," a change in administered prices depends on a specific entrepreneurial decision.[26] In making decisions, sellers with discretionary power use pricing rules or formulas which provide a restraining influence.

The most well known is the rule of "target return pricing" popularized by Lanzillotti and by Eckstein and Fromm.[27] It holds that a firm first determines the "standard volume," or most likely rate of operation, and a "target," or desired rate of return on investment. It then estimates a "standard" unit labor and unit materials

---

[25] G. Stigler and J. Kindahl, *The Behavior of Industrial Prices* (New York: National Bureau of Economic Research, 1970). Of the sixty-four commodities in their study, only twenty-three showed declines during the recessions according to the Bureau of Labor Statistics. Forty showed declines when actual transactions prices were used.

Further research on the accuracy of the wholesale price index is currently being carried out by Robert Gordon at the National Bureau of Economic Research. Gordon has found that wholesale prices for durable goods are far more flexible than Stigler and Kindahl observed for staple industrial materials and that the WPI is biased upward to a greater extent at low capacity rates than at high capacity rates. In a preliminary manuscript of the study entitled "The Measurement of Durable Goods Prices" the author reports that "if utilization increases from .75 to .90 during a business cycle expansion, the ratio of transactions to list prices rises by about four percent." He also discusses evidence produced by other researchers on biases in the WPI resulting from failure to account for quality changes. "Chow found that the quality corrected price of computers [one of our more concentrated industries] fell by 20 percent *per year* relative to the official index during 1954-65, and Kravis-Lipsey found an 11.4 percent annual rate of decline relative to the WPI during 1957-64." It would appear that the rate of price increase in concentrated industries derived from WPI statistics is considerably overstated. Perhaps it is more overstated for the concentrated industries than the nonconcentrated.

[26] However, a specific entrepreneurial decision is also required in atomistic industries. See G. C. Archibald, "Large and Small Numbers in the Theory of the Firm," *Manchester Journal of Economics and Social Studies*, January 1959, pp. 104–9; K. J. Arrow, "Toward a Theory of Price Adjustment," *The Allocation of Resources* (Stanford: Stanford University Press, 1959).

[27] Robert Lanzilotti, "Pricing Objectives in Large Companies," *American Economic Review*, vol. 48 (December 1958), pp. 921–40; Otto Eckstein and Gary Fromm, "The Price Equation," *American Economic Review*, vol. 58 (December 1968), pp. 1159–83.

cost and adds to costs a margin enabling it to realize its target return when operating at the standard volume. The essence of the rule is that prices based on standard costs do not respond directly to changes in operating rates, actual costs, or demand. Rather, they respond to changes in standard costs.[28]

Initial adjustments by oligopolists to fluctuating demand are supposed to be in terms of rate of output or the level of inventories. Prices are affected only when attempts by all firms to expand (or contract) output affect the demand for labor and materials. Input prices are thought to be more flexible and to adjust immediately. They are translated to standard costs in the pricing formula and then to selling price. The length of time required for the translation accounts for the lag in adjusting prices in concentrated industries.

The problem with this hypothesis is that it sees market imperfections predominately where sellers are few. It ignores a more basic source of imperfection, the cost of information about market conditions. All prices in the economy are set or changed as a result of a decision made by some individual, even in markets as perfect as the securities and commodities exchanges. Prices are changed as soon as new information on market conditions is received. The change is automatic only in the sense that failure to alter prices will cause the seller to earn less than he otherwise could. This is the situation in any market structure. The adjustment of prices will be faster when the receipt of information on costs and demand is rapid and not costly, that is, when the consequence of keeping the old price becomes known to the seller with less lag.

It is likely that some type of cost-based rule of thumb will be used in setting prices in all manufacturing industries, as well as in wholesale and retail trade regardless of the level of seller concentration. A rule of thumb can be viewed simply as a way of estimating the best price when a firm sells many products with joint costs, different demand elasticities, and limited information. The length of the response lag will be a function of how often the rule is revised in terms of the size of the "profit margin" and the estimate of standard costs. On both of these factors, however, the theory of target return pricing is silent. It admits that the target is ultimately based on demand but says little about how to determine it, when it should be revised, or when standard costs should be revised.

---

[28] In the theory of target return pricing outlined by Eckstein and Fromm, "price is altered if the cost of producing the standard output changes either because of changes in the price of direct inputs or because of technical progress. However, price will not respond to cost changes caused by changes in operating rates, or to changes in demand." "The Price Equation," p. 1165.

Factors affecting the last might be the frequency of input purchase and the degree to which productivity is closely monitored. No evidence has been offered to show that the frequency of input purchase is lower for the highly concentrated industries.

Furthermore, no explanation is given for the length of the lag. A lag of several months might be plausible in view of the imperfections created by collusion and difficulties in obtaining information. However, it has been argued that administered inflation lasted from 1953 to 1959 or longer, which would imply that many years were required for concentrated industries to translate the increase in demand fully into the price level.[29]

The empirical basis for applying the target return model to oligopoly has also been questioned. A study by Weston revealed a number of confusions resulting from a lack of understanding of accounting and financial planning effects on control processes in large firms.[30] The terms "standard volume" and "standard costs" are used by managers as a basis for analyzing accounting variances from such standards in their efforts to improve cost efficiency. The variances are carried over into actual costs when each period's accounting reports are drawn up, generally quarterly or monthly. Rather than being a cause of lagged adjustments, standards enable managers to anticipate market changes. Once the nature of cost control is understood, it is hard to imagine that oligopolistic firms would take several years to react to or to catch up with market demand.

Price Rigidity among Atomistic Sellers. The existence of rigid prices has led some to believe that traditional economic theory is unsuited to explain price behavior in a modern economy. Armen Alchian, however, has offered an alternative explanation for the inflexibility of prices within the framework of traditional theory.[31] He views the maintenance of stable prices as a method of reducing the search costs of buyers. If sellers were to adjust price continuously in response to fluctuations in demand, buyers would be forced to search for an acceptable purchase price each time a purchase was to be made. They would also have a difficult time predicting their own production costs in order to be able to negotiate with potential customers. Thus, sellers tend to maintain stable prices and output and to allow inven-

---

[29] James Dalton, "Administered Inflation and Business Pricing: Another Look," *Review of Economics and Statistics*, November 1973.

[30] Fred Weston, "Pricing Behavior of Large Firms," *Western Economic Journal*, March 1972, pp. 1–18.

[31] Armen Alchian, "Information Costs, Pricing, and Resource Unemployment," in E. S. Phelps, ed., *Microeconomic Foundations of Employment and Inflation Theory* (New York: W. W. Norton and Co., Inc., 1970), pp. 27–52.

tories and order back logs to fluctuate. Frequency of price change is therefore related to factors which determine the search cost of buyers and the costs to sellers of holding inventory and altering the rate of production.

Alchian illustrates his theory by pointing out that atomistic restaurant owners do not cut prices whenever the number of customers falls below normal. They maintain prices even though capacity is excessive. Prices could be adjusted daily or hourly so that the restaurant was always operating at full capacity. The widely fluctuating prices would stabilize output. However, such frequent changes would force customers to compare prices of many competing restaurants before each meal, and the need to search would be a costly inconvenience. Consumers often prefer to pay a slightly higher price, which would be required if capacity were often excessive, in order to eliminate the cost of search. Therefore, rigid prices, idle capacity, and fluctuating output may be common to atomistic as well as oligopolistic sellers.[32]

Lag and Catch-Up. The theory of price rigidity as developed so far would predict that prices would not rise when demand increases. This hardly seems inflationary. Why is it claimed that price rigidity is related to inflation? The answer is that rigid prices, which do not rise when demand increases, do not fall when demand decreases. The original failure of oligopoly prices to rise in response to an increase in demand produces what Galbraith has called "unliquidated monopoly gains."[33] It allows sellers to raise price and profits at some later date when demand is not rising. It may also allow oligopolists to maintain prices when demand falls. Once firms have failed to respond to a demand increase, there is always the possibility that they will increase prices at some later date, even though there has been no further change in market conditions. Viewed in the short run, such price increases appear to be spontaneous efforts to increase profits unrelated to current market changes.

The net result of rigid prices is to produce a situation in which price rises in concentrated industries lag behind other price increases during a business expansion. However, when aggregate demand stops rising or begins to contract, prices in concentrated industries rise more rapidly than prices in the rest of the economy. Whether or not

---

[32] Lester Telser, "When Are Prices More Stable than Purchase Rates?" *Revue d'Economie Politique*, vol. 81 (1971), pp. 273–301, translated and reprinted in Yale Brozen, ed., *The Competitive Economy* (Morristown: General Learning Press, 1974).

[33] Galbraith, "Market Structure and Stabilization Policy," p. 127.

oligopoly prices are inflationary depends on what phase of the business cycle is under consideration. During expansions, industrial concentration would retard the rate of inflation, but during a business contraction, the effect would be the opposite.

Secular Inflation. The theory outlined above suggests that industrial concentration affects the timing of price rises over the business cycle rather than the magnitude of the price rise. Therefore, in the long run, concentration would have no bearing on the rate of inflation. Some writers, however, suggest that industrial concentration imparts an upward bias even to the long-term rate of price change.

One argument is that high profits earned by concentrated industries become a target for union wage demands. But high profits in atomistic industries would seem to be equally attractive, unless the objection is raised that unions find atomistic industries more expensive to organize. Oligopolists are also said to be more generous or more susceptible to union pressure for wage increases, because any increase in cost resulting from high wages can be passed on to consumers by raising prices. It is generally believed that the price increases are usually more than enough to compensate for the higher wages. In fact, negotiated wage increases are said to provide a signal for industry-wide price increases in reponse to demand pressures which have built up over time. The actions of concentrated industries are thus thought to initiate a wage-price spiral with spillover effects to other industries which eventually produces a rise in the general price level.

The argument that oligopolistic sellers allow labor costs to increase more rapidly than do atomistic sellers is weak for several reasons. First, there is no empirical evidence to support the view that signal effects of wage increases are any greater where there are few sellers. Second, it is not true that the entire cost of a wage increase can be passed on to the consumer when demand is not being inflated.[34] The effect of raising prices will be fewer units sold. Lower output levels combined with the higher costs of production will mean that, given current demand, profits will be lower. Once a firm has set an optimal selling price, a wage increase and a price rise to offset added costs will only reduce profits.[35] Therefore, oligopolistic firms

---

[34] M. Burstein and W. Oi, "Monopoly Competition and Variability of Market Prices," *Metroeconomica*, vol. 12 (August-December 1960).

[35] It is theoretically possible that the entire cost could be passed on if marginal cost is rising and demand is close to unitary elasticity. The reduction in costs which results from decreased output may exceed the reduction in total revenue by enough to offset the added wage cost. However, this is very unlikely.

have as much incentive to resist union wage demands as atomistic firms. One could even argue that oligopolists are more likely to resist union demands because they have greater bargaining strength. In the process of industry-wide bargaining, a management coalition comprised of many atomistic firms is less able to restrain individual member firms from seeking separate agreements. Oligopolists, on the other hand, are likely to form stronger bargaining units.

A further objection to the wage-price spiral argument is that it offers no explanation as to how the higher wages and prices in oligopolies can spill over into nonoligopolistic industries. Presumably, firms in atomistic industries lack the ability to pass on wage increases and therefore are more resistant to union pressure. The effects of the spillover would thus be to increase the supply of labor to other industries and cause smaller wage increases. In other words, higher prices with wage increases in oligopolistic industries would reduce their rate of employment growth. Their output would expand more slowly, or the industry would become more capital intensive. Labor resources would then be released to move into atomistic industries, which would find their supply of labor growing rapidly. This increase in supply would retard the rate of wage increases. Therefore, even if oligopolists were more prone to raise wages, the behavior of prices and wages in atomistic industries would offset rather than reinforce such rises.[36]

Summary of Theory. Theoretical arguments have been presented on two distinct inflationary effects of industrial concentration. The first is a lag and catch-up effect, which purports to explain the timing of price increases — inflation. It predicts a slower rate of price increases for concentrated industries during the early stage of an inflationary process, followed by more rapid price increases in the later stages. The price behavior used to explain the catch-up theory is the imperfection of oligopolistic collusion and the prevalence of cost-determined pricing formulas, which make prices insensitive to demand. This theory may be countered by arguments that apparently rigid prices and cost-based rules of thumb exist in nonoligopoly industries and that the lags which may be produced are unlikely to extend over the five- to ten-year period "observed" by the proponents of the administered price thesis.

Several empirical tests of these theoretical arguments have been conducted to confirm the theory. The tests, in the form of regression studies, are analyzed below in Section 3. The results of further tests

---

[36] Steve Sobotka, *Profile of Michigan* (New York: Macmillan, 1962).

carried out by the author are presented in Appendix A; these latter are related only to the lag and catch-up effect of concentration.

A second alleged effect of concentration is the production of a secular inflationary bias in the economy. This view contrasts with the lag and catch-up theory, which maintains that only the timing of price changes and not their magnitude is affected by industrial concentration. The arguments for secular inflation also rest on the presumed ability of unions to obtain higher wage increases from concentrated industries and the tendency for oligopolists to be less active in instituting cost-saving production techniques. These counter-arguments ignore the incentives that oligopolists have to hold down costs in order to maintain or increase profits. The theoretical issues can only be resolved by empirical investigation. Unfortunately, there have been few analyses which focus directly on the behavior of costs in concentrated industries. In the hope of resolving the issue, evidence on long-term trends of productivity and labor costs is introduced in Section 4.

3. Prior Tests for Administered Inflation

Four very similar tests of the effects of industrial concentration were carried out in recent years: two of them for U.S. manufacturing industries by Leonard Weiss and James Dalton, one for EEC countries by Louis Phlips, and one for Canada by W. Sellekaertes and R. Lesage.[37] Each test was made on the basis of a cross-section regression of industry price changes on changes in unit labor cost, unit material costs, output, and industry concentration. The logic of these tests is that, after changes in costs and output (a proxy for demand) are accounted for, an effect for concentration can be considered as a verification of the administered inflation hypothesis. All authors except Phlips claimed to find support for the hypothesis, although Weiss's second study showed concentration to have a negative effect on prices in the late 1960s. The results of the various studies are summarized in Table 1. The regression coefficient gives the effect of concentration on price change. A positive effect would be considered evidence that concentration is inflationary.

[37] Leonard Weiss, "Business Pricing Policies and Inflation Reconsidered," *Journal of Political Economy*, vol. 74 (April 1966), pp. 180–81, and "The Role of Concentration in Recent Inflation," in Yale Brozen, ed., *The Competitive Economy*, pp. 204–10; James Dalton, "Administered Inflation and Business Pricing: Another Look"; W. Sellekaertes and R. Lesage, "A Reformulation and Empirical Verification of the Administered Prices and Inflation Hypothesis: The Canadian Case," *Southern Economic Journal*, January 1973, pp. 345–60; Louis Phlips, "Business Pricing Policies and Inflation — Some Evidence from EEC," *Journal of Industrial Economics*, vol. 43 (November 1969), pp. 1–14.

Table 1
FIVE REGRESSION STUDIES OF THE ADMINISTERED INFLATION HYPOTHESIS [a]

Author	Country	Time Period	Regressional Coefficient of Concentration [b]	Cost Variable [c]
Weiss (1966)[d]	U.S.	1953-59	.085 (2.50)	Unweighted cost
Weiss (1966)[d]	U.S.	1959-63	−.013 (.619)	Unweighted cost
Weiss (1971)[d]	U.S.	1963-68	−.042 (.894)	Unweighted cost
Weiss (1971)[d]	U.S.	1967-69	−.128 (3.20)	Cost variable excluded
Dalton (1973)	U.S.	1958-63	.112 (2.29)	Weighted cost
Dalton (1973)	U.S.	1963-66	−.0023 (.0632)	Weighted cost
Dalton (1973)	U.S.	1967-69	.053 (1.444)	Weighted cost
Sellekaertes and Lesage (1969)	Canada	1957-59	.119 (1.6)	Unweighted cost
Sellekaertes and Lesage (1969)	Canada	1959-61	.125 (2.3)	Unweighted cost
Sellekaertes and Lesage (1969)	Canada	1963-67	−.014 (−.1)	Unweighted cost
Phlips (1969)[d]	Belgium	1958-64	−.492 (3.09)	Weighted cost
Phlips (1969)[d]	Benelux	1958-64	−.090 (1.50)	Weighted cost

[a] The dependent variable in the regressions was price. The independent variables were unit labor and materials costs, output, and concentration. For full citations of studies, see footnote 36.

[b] Figures in parentheses are t-statistics.

[c] Some authors weighted each cost variable by the percentage of total costs for which it accounts.

[d] Studies by Weiss and Phlips reported standard errors rather than t-statistics. To facilitate comparisons with other studies, t-statistics were computed and are reported here.

22

Since the administered price thesis predicts opposite effects for concentration during periods of lag and catch-up, the effects could, at some point, offset each other. Therefore, any effect for concentration (positive, negative, or zero) can be viewed as consistent with the theory. It is only when related to a particular phase of the business cycle that a given effect lends support to the theory. The interpretation of test results is complicated, however, because neither the length of the lag nor its point of origin is well specified by the theory. The result is one can never be certain whether the period of analysis encompasses the effects of the lag, the catch-up, or some combination of the two.

Weiss's basic finding was a positive and statistically significant effect for concentration for the period 1953-59 and statistically insignificant or significant negative effects in all other periods. He argued that the 1953-59 positive effect was a "temporary delayed reaction to the great inflations of the 1940s."[38] The insignificant effect of concentration from 1959 to 1963 was interpreted as evidence that the catch-up from the 1940s was complete by 1959 and that no further lags occurred during the next four years. For the period 1963-68, Weiss found what he considered a statistically insignificant effect for concentration, while for the period 1967-69, he observed a significant negative effect.

One can conclude from Weiss's results that, during the entire quarter century from the mid-1940s through 1969, administered inflation occurred only from 1953 through 1959.[39] Weiss predicted, however, that because of the negative effects for the period 1967-69 "the result may be another administered inflation in the early 1970s."[40]

Another look at the administered inflation phenomenon in the United States was taken by Dalton, using the same data sources and covering some of the same time periods as Weiss. Whereas Weiss found an insignificant effect for concentration from 1959 to 1963, Dalton found a positive and significant effect for the years 1958-63 (Table 1). Dalton viewed his finding as consistent with the administered inflation hypothesis "since 1958-63 follows the inflationary years 1955-58, [and] concentration should have a positive effect during 1958-63 because of the catching up process."[41] Thus, the years

[38] Weiss, "Business Pricing Policies and Inflation Reconsidered," p. 186.

[39] While the statistical analysis carried out by Weiss used data from 1953 to 1969, his discussion of influences on price behavior extended back to the inflationary period of the 1940s.

[40] Weiss, "The Role of Concentration in Recent Inflation," p. 207.

[41] Dalton, "Administered Inflation and Business Pricing," p. 517.

1955-58 could be seen by one author (Dalton) as a "lag" period and by another (Weiss) as a catch-up.

For the years 1963-66, Dalton found a statistically insignificant effect, which (because of the negative value of the coefficient) was interpreted as evidence that administered prices were lagging behind other prices. For the period 1967-69 he observed a statistically significant positive effect for concentration (Table 1). His explanation for the differences between these periods was "that after the buildup of inflationary pressures during 1963-66, they (oligopolists) began adjusting prices upward, during 1967-69."[42]

Comparing the interpretations of these authors illustrates the equivocal nature of the administered inflation thesis. Both positive and insignificant effects for concentration were regarded as consistent with the administered inflation theory for the period 1958-63, while both positive and negative effects were considered as consistent for the period 1967-69. The two authors used almost identical time periods and data, observed opposite effects for concentration, and yet interpreted their results as consistent with the administered inflation hypothesis. Since any effect is regarded as evidence of the existence of administered inflation, there really is no evidence.

Sellekaertes and Lesage tested the influence of concentration on price change in three different time periods. They observed a positive significant effect in the first two periods, 1957-59 and 1959-61, and an insignificant effect in the last, 1963-67. The period 1961-63 was excluded from their study. The authors interpret their results as supporting the theories of Means, Galbraith, and Ackley. There are several inconsistencies, however, resulting from improper interpretation of cross-section results. The price relationships observed in cross-section studies are not the absolute but rather the relative changes in concentrated as opposed to nonconcentrated industries. In their explanation of the two periods of positive effect for concentration, the second is supposed to represent a catching up of what was lost in the first. But this interpretation would require that the first period show a negative effect for concentration rather than the reported positive effect. The third period should also show a negative effect since it supposedly represents a period when oligopolistic prices are lagging behind demand.

The last test for the existence of administered prices, by Phlips, found either an insignificant effect or statistically significant negative effects for concentration for the years 1958-64. He interpreted these

---

[42] Ibid, p. 519.

results as a contradiction of the administered inflation theory. Since he did not discuss the results in terms of lags or catch-ups, one may assume that in his interpretation of the administered inflation thesis the only effect of concentration is to raise prices, an effect which did not occur in the data he examined.

4. Empirical Evidence on Concentration and Inflation

Rates of price change for different levels of concentration in various periods between 1954 and 1973 are shown in Table 2. The table gives the average annual percentage price change for each of four industry groups, based on the four-firm industry concentration ratio for the year 1963. This ratio measures the percentage of industry sales accounted for by the four largest sellers. It is the most widely used measure of market concentration.

The price change for each industry was compiled and expressed as an average annual percentage change. Data are for the four-digit SIC industries that form the basis of the table and are given in Appendix B.

The most striking feature of Table 2 is the evidence that in none of the periods did prices in the high concentration groups rise significantly faster than in the low. For all periods but one, 1969-70, the average price rise for the highest concentration group was less than for the lowest group. Thus, it appears that for the entire period 1954-73 the average rate of price increase for the high concentration groups has been substantially less than for the low concentration groups.

This long-term pattern of price change contradicts directly the hypothesis that concentration creates a secular inflationary bias. If there were either evidence for that hypothesis, as a result of leniency toward union wage demands among oligopolies or failure to control costs, one would expect prices to increase fastest where concentration was highest. While this pattern could not continue indefinitely, one would expect to observe periods of considerable length when prices would go up faster in the concentrated industries. But this was not the case for the nineteen-year period between 1954 and 1973.

The period of price stability from 1958 through 1965, when prices rose by .42 percent per year, contrasts sharply with the period 1967-73, when prices rose by more than 5 percent per year. This difference is not due to any sudden change in industry structure. Such changes take place at a very slow rate. It is more likely due to differ-

Table 2
AVERAGE ANNUAL PERCENTAGE PRICE CHANGE BY LEVEL OF INDUSTRIAL CONCENTRATION FOR SELECTED TIME PERIODS, 1954-73

Four-Firm Concentration Ratios

Period	Less than 25 percent	More than 25 and less than 50 percent	More than 50 and less than 75 percent	More than 75 percent	All levels
	N = 131	N = 150	N = 76	N = 23	N = 380
(1) 1954-58	1.70 (.23)	1.79 (.22)	1.77 (.29)	1.58 (.67)	1.74 (.14)
	N = 65	N = 89	N = 59	N = 22	N = 235
(2) 1958-63	0.28 (.20)	0.40 (.16)	0.39 (.29)	−0.24 (.42)	0.31 (.12)
(3) 1963-66	1.98 (.29)	1.56 (.29)	0.86 (.27)	−0.28 (.71)	1.33 (.17)
(4) 1958-65	0.51 (.15)	0.54 (.14)	0.42 (.22)	−0.35 (.45)	0.42 (.10)
(5) 1966-69	2.89 (.33)	2.40 (.26)	2.59 (.36)	1.85 (.75)	2.53 (.18)
(6) 1969-70	2.81 (.72)	4.22 (.48)	4.03 (.58)	4.39 (1.29)	3.80 (.32)
	N = 20	N = 32	N = 26	N = 13	N = 91
(7) 1971-73	12.00 (3.16)	10.51 (2.58)	4.56 (1.00)	1.98 (.59)	7.91 (1.23)
(8) 1967-73	7.60 (1.44)	6.04 (.92)	4.54 (.50)	2.27 (.72)	5.41 (.51)

Note: N = the number of observations. Figures in parentheses are standard errors.

Source: Price change, rows 7-8: U.S. Bureau of Labor Statistics, Wholesale Price Index, Industry Sector Price Indexes; *Monthly Labor Review*, May 1974; *Handbook of Labor Statistics*, 1973. Price change, rows 2-6: U.S. Bureau of Labor Statistics, Wholesale Price Index, compiled for four-digit SIC industries by U.S. Department of Commerce, Bureau of Economic Analysis, and Federal Reserve Board (unpublished). Price change, row 1: U.S. Bureau of the Census, *Census of Manufactures, 1963*, vol. 4, "Census Unit Value Indexes." Four-firm concentration ratios: U.S. Bureau of the Census, *Concentration Ratios in Manufacturing Industry, 1963*, committee print of the Subcommittee on Antitrust and Monopoly, 89th Congress, 2d session (Washington, D.C.: U.S. Government Printing Office, 1966).

ences in government monetary and fiscal policies.[43] In fact, the experience of the first period demonstrates that price stability can be achieved by proper monetary and fiscal policy without any structural changes in industry. From 1958 through 1965, the stock of money grew at a 2.7 percent compound annual rate in contrast to a 6.3 percent annual rate from 1966 through 1973.

Comparing the period of price stability, 1958-65, with the period of inflation, 1967-73, reveals the same price pattern with respect to industrial concentration in both — a lower rate of price increase generally for the high concentration groups. There were no structural changes between inflationary and noninflationary periods, and there were also no basic differences in the behavior of prices under different rates of inflation.

The differences between rates of price increase are most dramatic for the most recent round of inflation. From 1971 to 1973 the annual rate of price increase was 12.0 and 10.5 percent for the two lowest concentration groups compared with 4.56 and 1.98 percent for the two highest. A pronounced negative correlation between the level of concentration and the rate of price increase prevailed in this period. One explanation for the degree of negative correlation may be the differential effects of the government wage-price controls which were instituted in August 1971. Violations of controls are less common among concentrated industries, perhaps because the small number of sellers makes detection much easier. With the removal of controls on all but the energy industries, it is probable that price rises in concentrated industries will exceed those in atomistic industries as prices catch up with increases in demand. This process of catching up will take some time because sellers cannot know immediately how much to increase prices after decontrol. A similar catching up probably took place in the period following the relaxation of the controls imposed during the Korean War. In fact, the so-called administered price inflation of the mid-1950s may have been no more than a catch-up of prices which had been held down during the period of price control. It seems clear that these "administered price inflations" are actually the result of the differential effects of price controls and not the exercise of discretionary power over price.

It is worthwhile noting the contrast between the policy of the Council of Economic Advisers from 1960 to 1968 — that inflation was administered by big corporations and powerful unions — and from 1969 to 1973 — that inflation was a consequence of demand

---

[43] The stock of money grew at an annual rate of 2.7 percent from 1958 to 1965 and at an annual rate of 6.3 percent from 1966 to 1973.

pull. The 1960-68 council laid down guidelines to be followed by big corporations and by unions for price and wage increases in the hope that inflation could be prevented in this way. It exerted pressure on the Federal Reserve to push money into the market to keep interest rates from rising as the demand for funds strengthened. As a consequence, an inflation momentum was built into the economy which would be enormously difficult to stem without causing a recession. The 1969-73 council exhorted the Federal Reserve to stop feeding money into the economy in 1969, in the hope that by cutting the money growth rate from 8 percent in 1968 to 3 percent by mid-1969 the economy would correct itself without a recession. But the Federal Reserve continued to contract money growth rates until the end of 1969, when they reached the 1 percent level, with the recession of 1970 as a consequence. During this period the wholesale price index did moderate its rise, going from an annual rate of 4.9 percent in 1969 to a rate of 2.7 percent in 1970. With price controls imposed in 1971, the Federal Reserve evidently thought the inflation-moderating job was done and it began again to increase the money growth rate until it reached 9.5 percent by the end of 1972, thus igniting more inflation.

Wage Rates, Productivity, and Unit Labor Cost. Evidence relevant to the behavior of labor cost in concentrated industries is presented in Table 3. Average annual percentage changes in production worker wages per man-hour (WMH), output per production worker man-hour (QMH), and total labor cost per unit of output (WSQ) have been computed for four-digit SIC industries in the concentration groups of Table 2. For these computations, the following data were obtained from *Industry Profiles* (1972) and from the Federal Reserve Board of Governors:

W_t = total production worker wages paid in year t,

WS_t = total wages and salaries paid in t,

MH_t = total production worker man-hours in t,

Q_t = FRB annual index of production .

Computations were made for the first six time periods of Table 2. The last two were omitted because data were not yet available. The subscripts 0 and 1 refer to beginning and end years of each period. Changes in labor cost variables were compiled as follows:

$$\text{Hourly wage rate } (WMH) = \frac{W_1}{MH_1} \Big/ \frac{W_0}{MH_0}$$

$$\text{Output per man-hour } (QMH) = \frac{Q_1}{MH_1} \bigg/ \frac{Q_0}{MH_0}$$

$$\text{Total unit labor cost } (WSQ)^{44} = \frac{WS_1}{Q_1} \bigg/ \frac{WS_0}{Q_0}.$$

The variables are expressed as annual percentage changes. If we look first at the growth of hourly wages (WMH), Table 3 shows a higher rate for the high concentration groups than for the low groups between 1958 and 1965. Superficially, these results may appear to support the notion that wage increases granted by oligopolists are generally inflationary. But this could only be the case if wages increased faster relative to productivity (QMH) in the concentrated industries than in the less concentrated. The data show that, except for the year 1969-70, QMH increased faster for the high concentration groups than for the low. The absolute growth of productivity, as well as the growth of productivity relative to wages, was higher for concentrated industries. Thus, with the exception of the year 1969-70, the higher growth in productivity for the high concentration groups prevented the growth in wage rates from being inflationary. It should be noted that, if the growth of productivity exceeds the growth of hourly earnings, then labor cost per unit of output (unit labor cost) will decline. It is the rate at which the unit labor cost rises, rather than wage rates or productivity, which directly influences the rate of price increase.[45]

The variable WSQ represents the change in total unit labor cost. Except for one year, 1969-70, WSQ has been lower for the high concentration groups than for the other groups. Thus, the behavior of this variable, too, contradicts the notion that concentrated industries have a tendency to permit inflationary wage increases.

The pattern of price behavior shown in Table 2 is explained by the behavior of wage rates, productivity and unit labor costs in

---

[44] The variable WS includes all forms of compensation such as salaries, wages, commissions, dismissal pay, all bonuses, and vacation and sick pay. It does not include employers' social security contributions or other nonpayroll labor costs such as employees' pension plans, group insurance premiums, and workmen's compensation. Since the factor used here is change in labor cost rather than level of cost, the exclusions will not affect the result as long as the ratio of excluded to included items is the same in base and current periods. Even if this ratio does change, if the change is the same for all levels of concentration, the bias introduced is likely to be very small.

[45] The measures of hourly wages (WMH) and productivity (QMH) used here pertain only to production workers, while the measure of total unit labor cost includes both production and nonproduction workers. Therefore, the change in unit labor cost shown in Table 3 is not exactly equal to the ratio of WMH and QMH.

Table 3

AVERAGE ANNUAL PERCENTAGE CHANGE IN WAGES, PRODUCTIVITY, AND UNIT LABOR COST BY LEVEL OF INDUSTRIAL CONCENTRATION, 1954-70

Four-Firm Concentration Ratios

Period	Less than 25 percent (N=138)			More than 25 and less than 50 percent (N=157)			More than 50 and less than 75 percent (N=78)			More than 75 percent (N=24)		
	WMH	QMH	WSQ	WMH	QMH	WSQ	WMH	QMH	WSQ	WMH	QMH	WSQ
1954-58	NA	4.05 (.34)a	1.57 (.26)	NA	4.59 (.29)	1.52 (.27)	NA	4.88 (.54)	1.52 (.48)	NA	6.16 (1.13)	0.70 (.83)
1958-63	2.69 (.08)	3.27 (.18)	−0.48 (.12)	3.03 (.11)	4.35 (.23)	−0.99 (.15)	3.35 (.16)	5.14 (.44)	−1.01 (.25)	3.73 (.13)	5.82 (.54)	−1.38 (.47)
1963-66	2.97 (.14)	3.99 (.38)	−0.16 (.34)	3.05 (.14)	3.68 (.45)	0.43 (.44)	3.57 (.31)	4.48 (.58)	−0.59 (.40)	3.05 (.26)	4.59 (1.60)	−0.73 (1.21)
1958-65	2.75 (.08)	3.68 (.21)	−0.54 (.14)	3.00 (.09)	4.46 (.28)	−0.72 (.19)	3.47 (.10)	5.56 (.50)	−1.00 (.24)	3.72 (.15)	6.38 (1.03)	−1.42 (.53)
1966-69	6.24 (.20)	2.95 (.45)	3.95 (.49)	5.86 (.22)	4.26 (.53)	2.86 (.56)	5.15 (.22)	2.61 (.51)	2.92 (.53)	5.65 (.25)	4.59 (.87)	1.51 (.82)
1969-70	4.67 (.62)	2.45 (.97)	4.37 (.97)	5.17 (.53)	0.78 (.87)	6.62 (.86)	6.49 (.84)	2.16 (.83)	5.82 (.95)	5.85 (.77)	−0.45 (1.63)	7.76 (1.83)

Note: The symbols used in the table are defined as follows: N = the number of observations, WMH = the hourly wage rate, QMH = output per man-hour, and WSQ = total unit labor cost.

[a] Figures in parentheses are standard errors.

Source: For 1954-58: U.S. Bureau of the Census, *Census of Manufactures, 1963*, vol. 4. For 1958-70: U.S. Bureau of the Census, *Industry Profiles, 1972;* and *Federal Reserve Bulletin,* July 1971, "Annual Index of Production."

Table 3. Relatively greater productivity in concentrated industries led to relatively lower unit labor costs and relatively lower price increases. During 1958-65, there were actually absolute declines in prices for the highest quartile of concentration compared to absolute increases for the lower quartiles. It appears that competition in concentrated industries forced sellers to lower their prices to pass on cost savings to consumers, despite rising prices in other industries. In other periods, there were only relative declines in prices for the concentrated industries because unit labor costs changes, while relatively lower, were still positive.

It will again be useful to contrast the period of price stability, 1958-65, with other periods, this time in regard to productivity. For all industry groups, productivity gains for the years 1958-65 exceeded wage gains. During the later periods, 1966-69 and 1969-70, productivity declined and the growth of wages accelerated. The result was inflation.

Table 3 also provides insight into the differential price behavior in concentrated industries which may appear to be a lag during expansions and a catch-up during recessions. Concentrated industries are generally more capital intensive[46] than nonconcentrated industries and experience the greatest gains in productivity during expansions and the greatest declines in productivity during recessions. Wage rates may not correspond to this pattern. The result will be a slower rise in unit labor costs (the ratio of wage rates and productivity) during business expansions and a more rapid rise during contractions. In other words, the differential behavior of unit labor costs produces a differential rate of price increase.

This difference in productivity growth can probably explain the higher rate of price increase observed in concentrated industries for the year 1969-70 (see Table 2). Table 3 shows that for this period wage increases were slightly higher for the highest concentration group than for the lowest. Productivity increase, on the other hand, was substantially lower for the former, so that the unit labor cost rose by 7.76 percent for the highest concentration group and only 4.37 percent for the lowest. The higher rate of price increase for this period can thus be related to the higher increase in unit labor cost.

Consumer Price Index. The above analysis of interindustry price change was based on the wholesale price index (WPI). It should be

---

[46] The coefficient correlation between capital intensity and four-firm concentration ratio for four-digit SIC industries is .444. S. I. Ornstein, J. F. Weston, and M. D. Intriligator, "Determinants of Market Structure," *Southern Economic Journal*, vol. 39 (April 1973), pp. 616.

noted, however, that the average rise in the WPI does not accurately reflect prices that consumers actually pay. One reason is the amount of double counting. Price rises in mining, for example, are counted in the increased prices of iron ore, raw steel, fabricated steel, and the final products made from steel such as cars and trucks. But only the rise in price of final goods directly affects consumer welfare. The real impact of inflation is more accurately reflected by the consumer price index (CPI), which counts price increases only once, in proportion to their weight in consumer budgets. The movements of individual commodities in the WPI are related to consumer welfare in that they are ultimately reflected in the CPI, but the weights assigned to each commodity in computing the overall WPI are not related to the commodity's importance in consumer budgets.

The CPI may mask the influence of industrial structure because the price effects of producer goods, in which there is much concentration, are spread out over numerous consumer products. That is, price rises in consumer products cannot always be traced to a particular group of producer prices. For example, an increase in the price of steel might ultimately raise the price of consumer products such as alcoholic beverages and processed fruits and vegetables because steel is used in the containers in which these products are sold. However, since a very small fraction of the total cost of such products is accounted for by steel, substantial increases in steel prices would cause only very small increases in their prices. On the other hand, increases in the prices of a wide range of manufactured products would ultimately produce visible price rises in these types of consumer goods. The total impact of concentration would be a function of the price rise in concentrated industries and the percentage of manufacturing value-added in consumer purchases. The consumer would also be affected by price increases going to those who sell capital goods and goods to government since he eventually must bear the cost.

If monopoly power becomes effective when the four largest firms in an industry account for 40 percent or more of sales, then about 41 percent of manufacturing value-added is subject to monopoly power.[47] Outside of manufacturing, industries are either relatively

---

[47] The 40 percent level is suggested by a merger guideline of the Justice Department which forbids mergers that result in a market share of larger than 10 percent. U.S. Department of Justice, "Merger Guidelines," May 30, 1968, pp. 1–27. If the four largest firms each had 10 percent, the four-firm concentration ratio would be 40 percent. The critical value of 40 percent is also suggested by Frederic M. Scherer, *Industrial Market Structure and Economic Performance*, p. 60. According to Scherer, 41.2 percent of the value-added in manufacturing for 1963 was produced in industries where the four largest firms accounted for more than 39 percent of the market.

nonconcentrated or regulated by government agencies. Manufacturing accounts for about 28 percent of GNP, which means that price increases due to high industrial concentration could influence only about 11.4 percent (.41 x .28) of total GNP. This suggests that even if all firms with monopoly power were raising their prices they could have only a small impact on overall prices paid by the consumer.

Table 4 shows the change in consumer prices during the recent inflationary period from 1967 through July 1973. It gives the percentage price increases for major items in the average consumer's budget. The items are arranged in groups which are likely to experience similar growth of demand.

In the category of housing, relatively small price increases occurred in the area of household appliances, which are the products of highly concentrated industries. Slightly greater price increases occurred for textiles and furniture, which are moderately concentrated. But the greatest increases of all items in the group occurred in the areas of domestic services and maintenance, which have the most atomistic structure.

A similar pattern is revealed in the area of transportation. The smallest increases were included in the prices of new automobiles, which are produced by highly concentrated industries. The largest increases were found in auto repair and maintenance, which are services performed predominantly by atomistic sellers.

It is interesting to note that those areas of housing and transportation which are subject to government regulation have also had very substantial price increases. Public transportation prices rose by 44.9 percent (despite, or perhaps because of, the Urban Mass Transit Assistance Program, which began in 1964),[48] while the average increase for all transportation prices was 24.8 percent. Property taxes were up by 52.6 percent, while the average of all housing costs rose by 34.2 percent.

The above pattern of price changes is also found in the area of food and apparel. The more concentrated manufacturing industries such as processed food and apparel have had the smallest price increases, while the atomistic industries such as agriculture (fresh fruit and vegetables) and apparel services have had the greatest price increases.

The area of health and recreation also presents some interesting comparisons. Drugs and prescriptions, which are relatively concen-

---

[48] *U.S. Statutes at Large*, 88th Congress, 2d session, 1964, vol. 78, P.L. 88-365, July 9, 1964, sec. 2, p. 302. See also George Hilton, *Federal Transit Subsidies* (Washington, D.C.: American Enterprise Institute, 1974).

Table 4

CHANGE IN CONSUMER PRICES BETWEEN 1967 AND JULY 1973

Category	Percentage Change
All items	32.7
Housing	34.2
Appliances (ranges, washer-dryers, refrigerators)	09.7
Fuel oil (No. 2)	30.8
Household textiles (sheets, curtains, bedspreads, pillows)	15.1
Household floor coverings (carpets, vinyl goods)	08.6
Household furniture (sofas, beds, chairs, tables)	25.9
Rent	24.3
Domestic service	46.2
Maintenance and repair services	58.0
Property taxes	52.6
Gas and electricity	25.5
Transportation	24.8
Automobile — new purchase	10.9
Gasoline	18.8
Auto repairs and maintenance	42.5
Insurance	38.1
Registration	23.7
Public transportation	44.9
Health and recreation	30.3
Recreational goods (TV, radio, camera, sporting goods)	09.4
Toilet goods (soap, powder, shaving cream, deodorant)	19.7
Drugs and prescriptions	05.9
Alcoholic beverages	22.8
Tobacco products	37.8
Hospital services	81.8
Personal care services (barber, beautician)	31.1
Physicians' and dentists' fees	37.5
Recreation services	33.2
Food	39.9
Processed fruits and vegetables	27.7
Other processed foods for home (fats, oils, sugars, beverages)	29.9
Meats, fish, and poultry	55.8
Dairy products	24.1
Fresh fruits and vegetables	61.3
Apparel and upkeep	25.8
Commodities, except footwear	25.2
Footwear	29.9
Apparel services	44.5

Source: U.S. Bureau of Labor Statistics, *The Consumer Price Index,* July 1973.

trated, have risen by only 5.9 percent, while physicians' and dentists' fees, which are atomistic, have gone up by 37.5 percent. Hospital service charges have gone up by over 81 percent. In the area of personal care, a comparison of toilet goods and the services of barbers and beauticians again provides an illustration of the smaller price increases occurring in concentrated industries. Toilet goods are a relatively concentrated industry, and prices rose by 9.4 percent. Personal care services are mainly offered by atomistic sellers, and their prices rose more than three times as much.

For food products, the average increase of all prices was 39.9 percent. For processed foods, however, the increases were under 30 percent. This finding should challenge the sometimes popular belief that increases in food prices result from the actions of middlemen who wish to increase their margin. The data of Table 4 suggest that the prices for the services of food processors rose more slowly than the prices for nonprocessed farm products.

5. Conclusion

Both theoretical and empirical evidence relating industrial concentration to inflation have been examined. The theoretical arguments were that concentration promotes inflation because it allows sellers to maintain prices when demand declines, to pass on inflationary wage increases, and to avoid competitive pressures to reduce costs. These arguments were found to be inconsistent with the evidence, which showed that prices and unit labor costs have increased more slowly in concentrated industries than in other industries. The main reason for the superior performance of firms in concentrated industries has been their greater gains in productivity. This finding suggests that the managers in these firms have been more successful in instituting cost-saving techniques of production.

This explanation for the difference in performance may be taken one step further: the expanded output of concentrated industries permits economies of scale in production. Firms in concentrated industries become more efficient as they grow larger. This explanation has important implications for the potential effects of deconcentration. Most important, the splitting up of large firms will reduce the overall growth of productivity in the economy because the newly created smaller firms will be less efficient. Deconcentration will therefore reduce the growth of real income, and it may even increase the rate of inflation as lower productivity generates higher prices.

Appendix A: Regression Models

A model for comparing past studies and conducting new tests can be developed as follows:

Let market price be determined by the following equation:

$$p_t = (\pi K_t + MC_t + SW_t)/Q_t \qquad (1)$$

where

$MC_t = $ total cost of materials used in time t

$SW_t = $ total wages and salaries paid in time t

$Q_t = $ quantity sold in time t

$K_t = $ capital stock in time t, defined as total operating assets with depreciation added back[49]

$\pi = $ normal rate of return on capital, defined as earnings before interest and depreciation, when capital is defined as above.

Thus, the industry price is equal to the sum of all costs, including normal profit, divided by output (that is, equal to long-run average cost). The term contained within the parentheses of equation (1) equals the value of shipments (VS). If the industry being considered is not competitive, then π in equation (1) could be greater than the normal rate, perhaps equal to the so-called target rate of return.

Price change between two points in time could then be calculated as follows:

$$\frac{p_1}{p_0} = \frac{\pi_1}{\pi_0} \cdot \frac{\pi_0 K_0}{VS_0} \cdot \frac{K_1}{K_0} \bigg/ \frac{Q_1}{Q_0} + \frac{MC_0}{VS_0} \cdot \frac{MC_1}{MC_0} \bigg/ \frac{Q_1}{Q_0} +$$
$$\frac{SW_0}{VS_0} \cdot \frac{SW_1}{SW_0} \bigg/ \frac{Q_1}{Q_0} \cdot \qquad (2)$$

Equation (2) makes price change a function of several components: change in profit rates $\dfrac{\pi_1}{\pi_0}$, unit labor cost $\dfrac{SW_1}{SW_0} \bigg/ \dfrac{Q_1}{Q_0}$, unit materials cost $\dfrac{MC_1}{MC_0} \bigg/ \dfrac{Q_1}{Q_0}$, and unit capital cost $\dfrac{K_1}{K_0} \bigg/ \dfrac{Q_1}{Q_0}$. Each

---

[49] Although one could argue that net capital assets are the proper measure to use, data on this type of assets are not available in a form adequate for testing. However, there is evidence that the measure of capital used for control purposes by large firms is gross capital assets rather than net capital assets. For a discussion of business pricing rules, see J. F. Weston, "Pricing Behavior of Large Firms," *Western Economic Journal*, March 1972, pp. 1–18, and Treasurer's Department, E. I. DuPont De Nemours and Company, "Executive Committee Control Charts," *AMA Management Bulletin*, no. 6 (1960). The regression equations computed below employ the change in capital stock between two points in time. As long as the ratio of net to gross capital remains the same in both periods, it does not matter which measure is used.

unit cost is weighted by its share of value of shipments in the base year. The weights for capital, materials, and labor are, respectively, $\frac{\pi_0 K_0}{VS_0}$, $\frac{MC_0}{VS_0}$, and $\frac{SW_0}{VS_0}$.

Past regression studies have estimated price change as a function of several of the components of equation (2), adding concentration as proxy for π_1/π_0. According to the administered inflation hypothesis, π_1/π_0 will be relatively lower for concentrated industries during a lag period and relatively higher during a catch-up. Therefore, the concentration ratio should have a negative sign when the computation is for a lag period and a positive sign for a period of catching up. It should be noted again that equation (2) represents an identity — it equates price change to cost change. When it is used as a basis for regression equations, however, one or more of the terms are excluded, and the concentration ratio is substituted for the excluded terms.

One major difference between the various earlier tests is the use of weighted or unweighted cost variables. The logic of weighting, as shown in equation (2), is that the unit cost variable influences the price only in proportion to its importance in total cost. For example, a given percentage change in unit labor cost would have a greater impact on price when the industry is labor intensive.

The explanatory cost variables used by Weiss and by Sellekaertes and Lesage were the unit materials cost and unit labor cost of equation (2). The weights as well as the cost of capital were excluded. Dalton and Phlips employed weighted cost variables but excluded the unit capital variable and also the weight of capital. While changes in capital costs may not be important in explaining short-run price changes, their exclusion may cause a bias for long-run computations. In either case, the bias caused by excluding capital cost is much greater when the weighted variables are employed. Because of the capital intensity of concentrated industries, the weights for labor and capital are, respectively, negatively and positively correlated with concentration. When both weights are excluded, the biases are opposite and possibly offsetting. However, when only the weight of capital is excluded, a net bias with respect to concentration remains. When the concentration ratio is introduced as a proxy for change in profits, it also acts as a proxy for the excluded weighted capital variable. Thus, concentration may appear to have a positive effect on price change when in fact it is only reflecting the influence of capital. This may explain why Dalton, using weighted variables, found concentration to be positive and statistically significant for the period 1958-63, while Weiss found it to be negative and insignificant.

Regression Equations. Table A-1 gives regression coefficients of concentration as estimated for 225 four-digit U.S. manufacturing industries for each of the twelve annual time periods between 1958 and 1970. The data sources are the same as in previous studies for the United States, except for an additional variable K_1/K_0, which was estimated from data on gross book value of depreciable assets and annual capital expenditures.[50] The weight of capital was estimated as the share of value of shipments which does not go to either labor or materials. Thus,[51]

$$\frac{\pi_0 K_0}{VS_0} = 1 - \left(\frac{MC_0 + SW_0}{VS_0} \right).$$

Each column of Table A-1 gives the regression coefficient for the concentration ratio (CON) in twelve time periods derived from a different specification of the regression equation. The variables that were included in each equation are given at the bottom of the table. Four different specifications are tested.

---

[50] Observations are based on four-digit SIC industries. Data for price change are derived from the Bureau of Labor Statistics, Wholesale Price Indexes. The series used in this study is an unpublished data set prepared by the Office of Business Economics (OBE) of the U.S. Department of Commerce. While the OBE computes indexes for all four-digit SIC industries, many are based on WPI commodity indexes which cover only a small portion of the total industry output. An industry was included in this study if at least 25 percent of its output was covered by the WPI commodity indexes. A similar standard was used by H. J. DePodwin and R. T. Selden, "Business Pricing Policies and Inflation," *Journal of Political Economy*, vol. 81 (April 1963), pp. 116–17, and by Leonard Weiss, "Business Pricing Policies and Inflation Reconsidered," *Journal of Political Economy*, vol. 74 (April 1966). The variables MC, SW, and VS were obtained from U.S. Bureau of the Census, *The Industry Profiles* (Washington, D.C.: U.S. Government Printing Office, 1972). Q_1/Q_0 is the Federal Reserve Index of Production, unpublished but described in the *Federal Reserve Bulletin*, July 1971. The variable CON is the four-firm seller concentration ratio from U.S. Bureau of the Census, *Census of Manufactures, 1967: Concentration Ratios in Manufacturing*, MC67 (S)-2-1 (Washington, D.C.: U.S. Government Printing Office, 1970); it was readjusted for regional and local markets on the basis of a study by D. Schwartzman and J. Bodoff, "Concentration in Regional and Local Industries," *Southern Economic Journal*, January 1971, pp. 343–48. Gross book value of depreciable assets *(GBVA)* may be found in U.S. Bureau of Census, *Annual Survey of Manufactures, 1964*, M64(AS)-6 (Washington, D.C.: U.S. Government Printing Office, 1967). Capital stock in each year was estimated from a base period GBVA by adding or subtracting the annual capital expenditures.

[51] Technically, this measure includes expenses besides profit, depreciation, and interest. It contains other overhead expenses such as rental payments, cost of sales branches, central administrative office costs, taxes, and advertising. It is assumed that these expenses change in proportion to K_1/K_0 for all levels of concentration.

In the first specification (column (1) of Table A-1), only the direct unit materials and unit labor costs are included in the regression. The unit capital cost and all the weights are excluded. The second specification (column (2) of Table A-1) is based on equation (2) and includes the unit labor, materials, and capital variables as well as their weights. Only the variable π_1/π_0 is excluded.

The results in column (3) of Table A-1 are computed from a respecification of equation (2) designed to focus more directly on π_1/π_0. In the first two specifications, the effect of concentration was tested by holding all of the other determinants of price change constant and including them as additional independent variables. An alternative to this method would be to subtract cost variables from both sides of the equation and regress the residual on concentration. This was done in the third specification for the direct labor and materials costs which could be subtracted without destroying the mathematical form of the equation. Thus, combining the materials and labor terms of equation (2) and subtracting them from both sides yields the following:

$$\frac{p_1}{p_0} - \left(\frac{MC_1 + SW_1}{VS_0} \bigg/ \frac{Q_1}{Q_0} \right) = \frac{\pi_1}{\pi_0} \cdot \frac{\pi_0 K_0}{VS_0} \cdot \frac{K_1}{K_0} \bigg/ \frac{Q_1}{Q_0} \cdot \quad (3)$$

Allowing π_1/π_0 to be function of concentration $(\pi_1/\pi_0 = (CON)^a)$ and taking logs of both sides of equation (3) gives:

$$\log \left(\frac{p_1}{p_0} - \frac{MC_1 + SW_1}{VS_0} \bigg/ \frac{Q_1}{Q_0} \right) = a \log CON + \log \left(\frac{K_1}{K_0} \right)$$
$$+ \log \left(\frac{\pi_0 K_0}{VS_0} \right) - \log \left(\frac{Q_1}{Q_0} \right) \cdot \quad (4)$$

In a regression fitted to equation (4), the coffiecient of log (CON) would be an estimate of a. These estimates are shown in column (3) of Table A-1. According to the lag hypothesis, the effect of concentration (that is, sign of a would be positive during catch-up periods and negative during lag periods.

In column (4) of Table A-1 the effect of concentration in all years is estimated simultaneously. When the effect is estimated for each year in a separate regression equation, there may be a loss of information on the impact of concentration in recession relative to the impact in expansion. One could argue that concentration always influences price in one direction (up or down) but that the influence is stronger in some periods. If so, the differential effects of concentration between time periods might become more apparent if they were estimated simultaneously. This has been done for column (4). For each industry there were twelve independent observations of price changes and cost changes. One regression equation was fitted to the entire data set (2,670 observations), allowing intercept dummies for the different time periods and a different slope for concentration in each period.[52] The different intercepts allowed for different rates of price change in all industries during different time periods. Thus, the effect of cost changes on price was assumed to be the same for all years, but the effect of concentration was allowed to be different.

Regression Results. In order to confirm the administered price hypothesis, the sign of the regression coefficients shown in Table A-1 should change between periods of lag and catch-up. However, there is little consistent evidence of this regardless of the equation employed. The periods 1960-61 and 1969-70 represent recession periods for which positive effects for concentration should be observed as prices rise more rapidly in order to catch up. However, in none of the columns of Table A-1 is the coefficient of concentration positive and statistically significant in either period. There are occurrences of sign reversals, but they do not appear to be related to the business cycle.

The results presented in Table A-1 provide little support for the administered price hypothesis. But more than that, they demonstrate the ambiguity in this type of analysis.[53] Even when annual time periods are used, there is overlap between lag and catch-up effects, thus leaving room for several interpretations. The results suggest that another approach should be tried. Since the supposed rigidity of prices with respect to demand is the heart of the administered inflation argument, a more fruitful approach might be to focus directly on the impact of changes in demand in concentrated and nonconcentrated industries.

Industry Demand. Prior studies have used the change in output, Q_1/Q_0, as a measure of the change in demand. However, this is unsatisfactory for two reasons. First, the change in industry output will always be due to the net effect of changes in both supply and demand, which typically act in opposite directions. That is, increases in wages and materials costs decrease the supply available at each

---

[52] One might argue that such a pooling of time series and cross section data will result in a problem of serial correlation. But since the data are, first, differences of price and cost, serial correlation is unlikely to occur.

[53] Previous studies have computed regression equations for periods covering several years. The periods were arbitrarily defined and, in at least one case, arbitrarily included some years and excluded other years. This method covers all years and allows the reader to determine whether the alternative effects for different years fit the administered inflation hypothesis.

Table A-1
REGRESSION COEFFICIENTS OF CONCENTRATION FOR TWELVE ANNUAL TIME PERIODS DERIVED FROM ALTERNATIVE ESTIMATING EQUATIONS, 1958-70

| Period | Dependent Variables | | | |
	Col. (1)	Col. (2)	Col. (3)	Col. (4)
1958-59	.010 (.010)[a]	.011 (.012)	−.046 (.038)	.019 (.011)
1959-60	−.002 (.010)	−.007 (.113)	−.050 (.047)	.004 (.011)
1960-61	−.010 (.011)	−.010 (.012)	−.006 (.039)	−.010 (.011)
1961-62	−.007 (.008)	−.009 (.009)	−.067 (.037)[b]	−.006 (.011)
1962-63	.001 (.012)	.011 (.013)	−.075 (.054)	−.005 (.011)
1963-64	−.016 (.009)[b]	−.024 (.010)[c]	−.015 (.032)	−.015 (.016)
1964-65	−.020 (.009)[c]	.006 (.009)	−.009 (.021)	−.010 (.011)
1965-66	−.023 (.009)[c]	−.012 (.010)	−.016 (.021)	−.023 (.011)[c]
1966-67	.013 (.011)	.004 (.012)	−.013 (.053)	.019 (.011)[c]
1967-68	−.015 (.009)	−.010 (.010)	−.032 (.016)[c]	−.007 (.011)
1968-69	−.027 (.012)[c]	−.017 (.013)	−.043 (.022)[c]	−.029 (.011)[b]
1969-70	−.009 (.012)	.007 (.013)	−.002 (.031)	.014 (.011)

Column (1): The estimating equation has the dependent variable of $\frac{p_1}{p_0}$. The independent variables are $\frac{SW_1}{SW_0} \Big/ \frac{Q_1}{Q_0}$, $\frac{MC_1}{MC_0} \Big/ \frac{Q_1}{Q_0}$, CON. A separate equation is estimated for each year.

Column (2): The estimating equation has the dependent variable of $\frac{p_1}{p_0}$. The independent variables are $\frac{SW_1 + MC_1}{VS_0} \Big/ \frac{Q_0}{Q_1}$, $1 - \left(\frac{MC_1 + SW_0}{VS_0} \right)$, CON. A separate equation is estimated for each year.

Column (3): The estimating equation has the dependent variable of log $\left(\frac{p_1}{p_0} - \frac{MC_1 + SW_1}{VS_0} \Big/ \frac{Q_1}{Q_0} \right)$. The independent variables are log $\frac{K_1}{K_0}$, log $\frac{Q_1}{Q_0}$, log $\left(1 - \frac{MC_0 + SW_0}{VS_0} \right)$, log CON. A separate equation is estimated for each year.

Column (4): The estimating equation has the dependent variable $\frac{p_1}{p_0}$. The independent variables are the same as those used in column (2) plus dummy intercepts and a different slope for concentration in each time period. The coefficients of concentration in all years are simultaneously estimated.

[a] Figures in parentheses are standard errors.
[b] Significant at the 10 percent level.
[c] Significant at the 5 percent level.

price (decreasing Q_1/Q_0), while increases in aggregate demand tend to raise industry demand (raising Q_1/Q_0). Second, the change in output will tend to be inversely correlated with price (which is contrary to the expected impact of demand) simply because the method of computing change in output involves deflating change in the value of shipments by the price index.

In order to properly account for shifts in demand, it is necessary to introduce a variable which is an exogenous influence on demand. Such a variable is the change in output not of the industry itself but of other industries which use the output in their own production processes. For the analysis below, the users of each industry's output were identified in *Input-Output Structure of the U.S. Economy, 1963*, 478 Level Table, which is predominantly concerned with four-digit SIC industries.

The assumption implicit in this approach is that, in the absence of changes in relative input prices, the proportion of the input factor in an industry's production process remains constant, so that the ex-ante ratio of each intermediate input factor to total output is the same in all years. For example, if the production of automobiles rises by 10 percent, it is assumed that the demand for steel by auto producers must also rise by 10 percent. If 20 percent of the steel industry's sales were purchased by the auto industry in the base year, increased auto production would increase the demand for steel by 2 percent. If we follow this logic, the increase in demand (DM_1/DM_0) for a given industry may be estimated by computing the weighted average change in output (Q_1/Q_0) of its consuming industries. The weights are dollar sales to each industry as recorded in the 1963 input-output study. The computation was made as follows:

$$DM_{1i}/DM_{0i} = (1/\Sigma_j a_{ij}) \cdot \Sigma_j a_{ij} \cdot Q_{1j}/Q_{0j}$$

where i denotes a producing industry, j denotes a consuming industry and a_{ij} refers to sales by producing industry i to consuming industry j. Since the assumption of a constant input factor is less valid for industrial output which goes to final demand (that is, consumption, investment, or government), computations were made only for those industries where intermediate sales account for more than 50 percent of total industry output.

According to the lag theory, current changes in demand have less impact on current price changes in concentrated industries than in nonconcentrated industries. This may be tested in two ways. One is to allow the demand variable, DM_1/DM_0, to have a different slope for different levels of industrial concentration. A larger and more significant slope for high levels of concentration would indicate support for the administered price thesis. The second is to allow an interaction between DM_1/DM_0 and CON. A significant interaction term would also indicate support for the thesis. The results are shown in Table A-2.

The regression equations in Table A-2 were computed for 101 industries in twelve time periods. This represents a combined sample of 1,212 separate observations on changes in price, cost, and demand. Combining time periods in the equations allowed for the possibility that cyclical fluctuations in aggregate demand may affect different industries at different points in time. It also allowed for the effect of shifts in consumer preferences, which reinforce or counteract cyclical fluctuations. Thus, the impact of demand from several sources was simultaneously considered.

In equation (1) of Table A-2 the cost variables of equation (2), p. 37, were included and the impact of DM_1/DM_0 was tested for all industries. While DM_1/DM_0 has high statistical significance (above .01) and takes on the correct sign, its magnitude is quite low. Its elasticity with respect to price change is only .05. Thus, demand does not seem to be an important variable in explaining price changes for all industries. One explanation may be that cost responses to demand changes occur after a rather short lag, so that annual price changes mainly reflect supply shifts. This could be true for all industries. However, according to the lag and catch-up hypothesis of administered inflation, it takes several years for prices in concentrated industries to catch up with demand. Thus, annual price changes would be appropriate for a test.

In equation (2) of Table A-2, although different slopes were allowed for different levels of concentration, the computed slopes turn out to be the same for all levels of concentration. The interaction term $(DM_1/DM_0) \cdot CON$ was entered in equations (3) and (4) of Table A-2 and turned out to be insignificant in both cases.

These regression results suggest that demand has equal impact on price changes regardless of the level of industrial concentration.

Table A-2
REGRESSION ANALYSIS OF CHANGES IN PRICE, COST, AND DEMAND, 1958-70

Equation	Constant	DC	OH	$\dfrac{DM_1}{DM_0}$	$D1 \cdot \dfrac{DM_1}{DM_0}$	$D2 \cdot \dfrac{DM_1}{DM_0}$	$D3 \cdot \dfrac{DM_1}{DM_0}$	$\dfrac{DM_1}{DM_0} \cdot CON$	R^2	N[a]
(1)	.559	.416 (.016)[b]	.343 (.018)	.047 (.020)					.342	1,212
(2)	.559	.416 (.017)	.342 (.019)		.047 (.021)	.046 (.021)	.046 (.021)		.342	1,212
(3)	.559	.416 (.017)	.342 (.019)	.046 (.021)				.002 (.005)	.342	1,212
(4)	.613	.409 (.017)	.332 (.018)					.004 (.005)	.339	1,212

$D1 = 1$ when $CON > 60$
$D2 = 1$ when $30 \leqq CON \leqq 60$ } and zero otherwise.
$D3 = 1$ when $CON < 30$

$DC = \left(\dfrac{MC_1 + SW_1}{VS_0} \bigg/ \dfrac{Q_1}{Q_0} \right) = $ (combined last two terms of equation (2), p. 37; direct costs)

$OH = \left(1 - \dfrac{MC_0 + SW_0}{VS_0} \right) \cdot \left(\dfrac{K_1}{K_0} \bigg/ \dfrac{Q_1}{Q_0} \right) = $ first term of equation (2) in text; overhead costs)

$DM_1 / DM_0 = (1/\Sigma a_{ij}) \cdot \sum_j a_{ij} \cdot (Q_{1j} / Q_{0j})$

[a] The sample contains observations on price change, cost change, and demand change in twelve annual time periods between 1958 and 1970 for 101 industries. Thus the total number of observations is $12 \times 101 = 1,212$. The equations referred to are on p. 37.
[b] Figures in parentheses are standard errors.

Appendix B

Table B-1
AVERAGE ANNUAL PERCENTAGE PRICE CHANGES
BY INDUSTRY GROUPS, 1954-73

SIC Description	1954-58 (1)	1958-63 (2)	1963-66 (3)	1958-65 (4)	1966-69 (5)	1969-70 (6)	1971-73 (7)
Industries with Concentration Ratios Less than or Equal to 25 Percent							
2013 Meat processing plants	1.6	—3.7	9.8	—.9	2.0	2.6	26.6
2015 Poultry dressing plants	—4.3	—2.6	3.5	—1.6	.3	—1.3	29.1
2021 Creamery butter	—.9	.2	4.8	.5	1.9	4.3	8.2
2026 Fluid milk	.9	2.6	1.8	1.7	3.8	2.4	
2033 Canned fruits and vegetables	.8	.7	1.6	.8	2.9	2.2	5.3
2036 Fresh or frozen packaged fish	9.0	.7	4.8	.3	3.3	5.8	20.9
2037 Frozen fruits or vegetables	1.0	2.9	—3.6	.5	1.5	3.2	
2042 Prepared feed for animals and fowl	—1.6	1.2	1.8	.7	—2.0	2.3	
2051 Bread, cake, and related products	2.2	1.7	2.3	1.2	2.3	5.3	
2071 Confectionary products	.5						
2086 Bottled and canned soft drinks	3.2						
2094 Animal and marine fats and oils	2.8	—3.6	7.9	.3	—3.9	18.8	58.1
2099 Food preparations, n.e.c.[a]	—3.7						
2241 Narrow fabric mills	1.1						
2252 Hosiery, n.e.c.	.3						
2253 Knit outerwear mills	.4						
2256 Knit fabric mills	—.9	—2.1	—2.6	—1.2	2.0	—13.9	
2272 Tufted carpets and rugs	—5.3	—1.8	—2.4	—2.0	—1.8	—1.6	2.3
2281 Yarn mills, except wool	—1.0	.5	.7	—.5	—.9	—2.0	
2311 Men's and boys' suits and coats	.9	1.5	3.4	2.1	5.9	6.7	4.4
2321 Men's dress shirts and nightwear	.9	1.3	1.2	1.1	3.1	3.4	3.3
2323 Men's and boys' neckwear	1.9	.0	.0	.0	5.7	12.0	
2327 Men's and boys' separate trousers	—.7	—.2	1.3	.2	1.7	1.2	—.2
2329 Men's and boys' clothing, n.e.c.	1.3						
2331 Women's and misses' blouses and waists	.9	1.4	.3	1.2	2.1	1.7	
2335 Women's and misses' dresses	1.1	.0	.0	.0	3.3	5.8	
2337 Women's and misses' suits and coats	—1.0	.7	2.3	1.4	3.1	6.2	
2339 Women's and misses' outerwear, n.e.c.	—1.6						
2341 Women's and children's underwear	—1.3	.4	.7	.4	1.9	1.5	
2351 Millinery	—1.1						
2361 Children's dresses and blouses	—.3						
2363 Children's coats and suits	—2.0						
2369 Children's outerwear, n.e.c.	—3.0						
2371 Fur goods	.3	—3.7	2.6	—2.6	—1.4	—3.6	

Table B-1 (continued)

SIC Description	1954-58 (1)	1958-63 (2)	1963-66 (3)	1958-65 (4)	1966-69 (5)	1969-70 (6)	1971-73 (7)
2384 Robes and dressing gowns	—.8						
2385 Waterproof outergarments	—.9						
2387 Apparel belts	4.8						
2389 Apparel and accessories, n.e.c.	2.9						
2391 Curtains and draperies	—1.1						
2392 House furnishings, n.e.c.	.3						
2394 Canvas products	—.6						
2397 Schiffli machine embroideries	—1.1						
2399 Fabricated textile products, n.e.c.	—2.5						
2411 Logging camps and contractors	1.5						
2421 Sawmills and planning mills, gen.	.2	.2	2.5	.3	11.2	—14.2	
2426 Hardwood dimensions and flooring	.5	.7	8.2	2.1	2.4	—.9	22.9
2429 Special product sawmills, n.e.c.	2.1						
2431 Millwork	.1	1.0	2.5	1.6	7.0	—1.9	
2432 Veneer and plywood	—1.4	—1.4	—.1	—1.2	6.7	—13.2	
2433 Prefabricated wood	.5	1.2	1.9	1.4	6.7	—1.5	
2499 Wood products, n.e.c.	.0	.3	4.5	1.7	7.5	—11.6	
2511 Wood furniture, not upholstered	2.3	1.3	2.3	1.3	4.7	3.5	
2512 Upholstered household furniture	.1	1.2	1.8	1.2	4.6	3.2	
2514 Metal household furniture	1.9	.4	—.2	.0	2.1	1.9	
2531 Public building furniture	2.5						
2541 Wood partitions and fixtures	2.3						
2542 Metal partitions and fixtures	5.4						
2599 Furniture and fixtures, n.e.c.	—1.0						
2643 Bags, except textile bags	3.3	—2.4	5.5	—.4	—.1	8.5	
2651 Folding paperboard boxes	3.3	—1.2	.5	—.9	1.0	.7	
2652 Setup paperboard boxes	.3	1.8	1.7	1.5	3.8	4.2	
2653 Corrugated shipping containers	2.9	.1	.0	—.3	2.8	3.0	
2711 Newspapers	1.9						
2731 Book publishing and printing	.4						
2732 Book printing	.6						
2751 Commercial printing, except lithograph	1.4						
2752 Commercial printing, lithograph	1.2						
2789 Bookbinding and related work	1.5						
2791 Typesetting	1.5						
2793 Photoengraving	1.5						
2834 Pharmaceutical preparations	—3.2	—1.2	—.4	—.9	.1	1.5	
2851 Paints and allied products	2.6						
2872 Fertilizers, mixing only	1.3	.6	.7	.6	—2.5	3.2	5.6
2899 Chemical products, n.e.c.	—.1						
2951 Paving mixtures and blocks	2.8	.0	—.2	.0	1.8	—.9	

Table B-1 (continued)

SIC	Description	1954-58 (1)	1958-63 (2)	1963-66 (3)	1958-65 (4)	1966-69 (5)	1969-70 (6)	1971-73 (7)
3069	Fabricated rubber products, n.e.c.	—.3	—.9	.1	—.9	4.2	4.4	
3079	Miscellaneous plastic products, n.e.c.	—3.2						
3111	Leather tanning and finishing	.7	1.6	6.7	2.2	—.2	—3.6	21.4
3131	Footwear cut stock	1.4						
3141	Shoes, except rubber	.6	2.2	2.9	1.9	4.2	3.7	
3142	House slippers	—1.0	1.0	4.2	1.3	5.4	2.0	
3151	Leather gloves and mittens	2.6						
3171	Women's handbags and purses	2.6						
3199	Leather goods, n.e.c.	1.1						
3251	Brick and structural tile	3.8	1.4	1.6	1.3	3.4	4.2	5.4
3271	Concrete block and brick	2.5	.1	1.6	.5	2.9	5.3	7.1
3272	Concrete products, n.e.c.	4.8						
3273	Ready-mixed concrete	2.9	.4	.4	.3	3.1	5.9	4.3
3281	Cut stone and stone products	—4.2						
3295	Minerals, ground or treated	3.0						
3323	Steel foundries	5.4	.8	.6	.7	3.7	4.7	
3362	Brass, bronze, and copper castings	5.1						
3369	Nonferrous castings, n.e.c.	2.5						
3399	Primary metal industries, n.e.c.	3.2						
3423	Hand and edge tools, n.e.c.	6.0	1.6	2.6	1.8	2.8	13.1	4.5
3433	Heating equipment, except electrical	2.1	—.8	—.1	—.7	1.7	5.0	
3441	Fabricated structural steel	6.2	—.6	3.7	.4	2.5	6.1	
3442	Metal doors, sash and trim	—.1	—2.1	.9	—1.5	2.6	7.3	
3443	Boiler shop products	5.8						
3444	Sheetmetal work	4.5	.1	1.3	.4	.4	5.0	
3449	Miscellaneous metalwork		—1.5	.7	—1.0	1.1	4.1	
3451	Screw machine products	3.9						
3452	Bolts, nuts, rivets, and washers	5.6	3.7	2.2	3.1	6.4	7.0	
3471	Plating and polishing	4.3						
3479	Metal coating, engraving, etc.	4.2						
3481	Miscellaneous fabricated wire products	3.0	—.8	1.1	—.3	1.7	6.2	
3494	Valves and pipe fittings	5.5	1.1	2.0	.4	4.1	7.3	
3498	Fabricated pipe and fittings	6.1	—.3	2.7	.3	6.8	4.8	3.9
3499	Fabricated metal products, n.e.c.	4.2						
3533	Oilfield machinery	4.0	.4	.8	.4	5.3	6.1	4.1
3541	Machine tools, metal-cutting types	2.4	2.2	5.1	2.9	4.5	6.1	
3542	Machine tools, metal-forming types	4.9						
3544	Special dies, tools, jigs, and fixtures	3.1						
3545	Machine tools accessories	5.8	3.4	3.2	3.0	4.5	5.0	
3548	Metalworking machinery, n.e.c.	3.4	2.1	3.0	2.2	4.5	—2.3	
3551	Food products machinery	7.6						

SIC Description	1954-58 (1)	1958-63 (2)	1963-66 (3)	1958-65 (4)	1966-69 (5)	1969-70 (6)	1971-73 (7)
3565 Industrial patterns	4.5						
3566 Power transmission equipment	7.1	2.5	3.3	2.8	3.3	8.0	
3585 Refrigeration machinery	—2.0						
3589 Service industry machines, n.e.c.	2.7						
3599 Miscellaneous machinery, except electrical	2.8						
3642 Lighting fixtures	2.3	.4	.6	.3	1.6	4.3	
3644 Noncurrent-carrying wiring devices	3.4	.0	2.0	.2	5.7	12.9	
3713 Truck and bus bodies	6.4						
3732 Boat building and repairing	5.1						
3791 Trailer coaches	1.3						
3799 Transportation equipment, n.e.c.	5.3						
3821 Mechanical measuring devices	5.4						
3941 Games and toys	1.1	—.2	.2	—.1	3.8	4.3	2.4
3961 Costume jewelry	.1	1.1	1.8	—.1	1.1	—3.3	
3962 Artificial flowers	.1						
3993 Signs and advertising displays	2.5						

Industries with Concentration Ratios Greater than 25 Percent and Less than or Equal to 50 Percent

SIC Description	1954-58 (1)	1958-63 (2)	1963-66 (3)	1958-65 (4)	1966-69 (5)	1969-70 (6)	1971-73 (7)
2011 Meat slaughtering plants	2.1	—2.8	6.6	—.8	2.3	1.5	22.7
2022 Cheese, natural and process	.3	1.6	8.6	1.8	3.7	6.0	
2023 Condensed and evaporated milk	.4	.5	4.9	.4	3.4	6.4	
2024 Ice cream and frozen desserts	—.8	.2	1.7	.2	2.3	2.4	
2031 Canned and cured seafood	2.0	.1	6.4	.6	2.5	9.4	
2034 Dehydrated food products	5.9	—2.0	.0	—2.0	7.7	3.7	
2035 Pickles, sauces, salad dressing	1.1	—1.9	6.4	—.1	2.5	7.8	
2041 Flour and other grain mill products	—2.0	1.5	4.3	1.8	—1.5	5.1	
2044 Rice milling	.5	—.6	—1.8	—1.2	—.6	.1	54.7
2061 Raw cane sugar	1.9	5.8	—4.5	1.1	—1.0	19.0	10.1
2082 Malt liquors	.4	.1	.4	.1	1.6	2.8	.6
2083 Malt	—1.0	.8	3.3	1.9	2.2	.8	11.6
2084 Wines, brandy, and brandy spirits	.5	1.4	—.1	1.2	2.0	3.0	7.1
2091 Cottonseed oil mills	—3.6	—1.4	6.4	—.8	—7.4	20.4	29.6
2092 Soybean oil mills	—5.3	1.5	7.0	2.3	—5.4	17.8	65.8
2096 Shortening and cooking oils	—2.0	—2.8	6.5	—.1	—.3	10.0	10.8
2098 Macaroni and spaghetti	.0	1.2	2.5	1.3	2.1	3.0	9.5
2211 Weaving mills, cotton	—.7	.4	.9	.4	1.4	2.6	
2221 Weaving mills, synthetics	—2.2	—.6	—1.7	—.3	4.8	—8.6	
2251 Women's hosiery, except socks	—4.7	—1.2	—1.7	—1.3	1.2	—2.4	
2254 Knit underwear mills	1.4	.6	.7	.6	2.7	1.9	2.8
2259 Knitting mills, n.e.c.	2.4	—.3	.6	—.1	3.3	.7	
2261 Finishing plants, cotton	1.2	.8	2.1	1.0	3.1	4.7	

Table B-1 (continued)

SIC Description	1954-58 (1)	1958-63 (2)	1963-66 (3)	1958-65 (4)	1966-69 (5)	1969-70 (6)	1971-73 (7)
2262 Finishing plants, synthetics	—.2						
2269 Finishing plants, n.e.c.	.1						
2279 Carpets and rugs, n.e.c.	—.7						
2282 Throwing and winding mills	—2.6						
2283 Wool yarn mills	—4.0						
2292 Lace goods	—3.1						
2293 Padding and upholstery filling	—1.5						
2294 Processed textile waste	4.1						
2295 Coated fabric, not rubberized	.5						
2298 Cordage and twine	—1.6	3.6	—.1	3.5	.4	5.1	
2299 Textile goods, n.e.c.	—.5						
2322 Men's and boys' underwear	1.9	.3	.2	.2	2.8	2.4	4.3
2328 Men's and boys' working shirts	.6	1.0	.8	.7	3.2	4.2	4.6
2342 Corsets and allied garments	1.1						
2352 Hats and caps	2.6						
2381 Fabric dress and work gloves	4.4	3.6	—.2	2.5	6.4	4.1	10.3
2386 Leather and sheep-lined clothing	2.9						
2393 Textile bags	1.5						
2441 Nailed wooden boxes and shook	.0						
2442 Wirebound boxes and crates	2.4						11.1
2443 Veneer and plywood containers	7.2						
2445 Cooperage	1.4						
2491 Wood preserving	.5						
2515 Mattresses and bedsprings	.6	.9	.1	.6	2.8	.4	2.6
2519 Household furniture, n.e.c.	1.2						
2521 Wood office furniture	1.3	1.2	2.6	1.3	6.1	4.6	3.8
2522 Metal office furniture	5.8	.0	.3	.1	3.9	6.8	
2591 Venetian blinds and shades	5.5						
2611 Pulpmills	1.5	—1.9	2.2	—.5	.0	9.4	
2621 Paper mills, except building paper	2.3	.3	2.0	.6	3.2	4.7	
2631 Paperboard mills	1.8	—1.1	.9	—.5	—1.1	.3	
2641 Paper coating and glazing	1.1						
2642 Envelopes	3.3						
2644 Wallpaper	.4						
2645 Die-cut paper and board	—1.4						
2661 Building paper and board mills	2.2	—1.2	—1.4	—1.5	2.7	—1.0	
2721 Periodicals	1.5						
2741 Miscellaneous publishing	2.4						
2753 Engraving and plate printing	1.3						
2761 Manifold business forms	1.6						
2782 Blank books and looseleaf binders	1.5						
2794 Electrotyping and stereotyping	1.6						

SIC Description	1954-58 (1)	1958-63 (2)	1963-66 (3)	1958-65 (4)	1966-69 (5)	1969-70 (6)	1971-73 (7)
2819 Industrial inorganic chemicals, n.e.c.	.6	1.4	1.5	1.5	1.1	3.3	
2821 Plastics material and resin	—2.3						
2831 Biological products	—3.4						
2842 Polishes and sanitation goods	1.5						
2843 Surface active agents	—1.4						
2844 Toilet preparations	1.6	.8	1.0	.7	2.9	1.9	
2871 Fertilizers	1.2	.5	2.8	.9	—2.5	—7.0	2.3
2891 Adhesives and gelatin	.8	—1.8	.8	—1.0	1.6	6.5	
2893 Printing ink	2.2						
2911 Petroleum refining	—.8	—.6	.7	—.6	.0	.6	18.6
2952 Asphalt felts and coatings	—.1	—1.5	1.9	—.7	.9	—1.4	
2992 Lubricating oils and greases	4.3	3.2	.1	2.3	.1	.0	
3161 Luggage	1.0						
3172 Small leather goods	.6	1.7	—.2	.8	.1	8.4	
3231 Products of purchased glass	2.8						
3241 Cement, hydraulic	4.1	.2	.0	.1	4.1	4.7	5.1
3253 Ceramic wall and floor tile	1.6	.4	—.5	.0	1.6	.9	
3255 Clay refractories	7.5	.3	1.7	.8	4.3	11.0	3.8
3259 Structural clay products, n.e.c.	4.9	1.4	.9	1.3	1.6	4.3	1.5
3264 Porcelain electrical supplies	3.1						
3274 Lime	1.8	1.3	.7	1.2	1.2	3.7	
3293 Gaskets and insulations	1.8						
3297 Nonclay refractories	5.4						
3299 Nonmetallic products, n.e.c.	5.8						
3312 Blast furnaces and steel mills	5.5	.1	1.0	.3	2.7	7.0	4.4
3315 Steel wire and drawing	5.1	—.4	.6	—.1	1.9	6.3	6.4
3316 Cold finishing of steel shapes	6.6	.4	.8	.4	3.7	6.9	3.3
3317 Steel pipe and tubes	6.8	—.2	.0	—.2	2.5	5.1	5.2
3321 Gray iron foundries	2.6	.9	1.9	1.1	3.7	5.4	
3322 Malleable iron foundries	4.3						
3341 Secondary nonferrous metals	—1.0	1.2	8.4	4.2	3.2	8.2	
3351 Copper rolling and drawing	—.2	.7	10.3	3.2	8.8	9.4	9.2
3356 Nonferrous rolling and drawing, n.e.c.	—1.0						
3357 Nonferrous wire-drawing, etc.	.4	.4	7.8	2.4	3.7	12.3	
3361 Aluminum castings	.9						
3391 Iron and steel forgings	5.8	.8	1.6	1.0	3.8	4.7	
3425 Handsaws and saw blades	8.1	1.4	.2	1.0	1.8	1.7	
3429 Hardware, n.e.c.	4.4	.3	1.5	.3	2.5	—.4	
3431 Metal plumbing fixtures	—3.5	—.5	—1.5	—1.1	2.3	3.0	4.9
3432 Plumbing fixtures and brass goods	—.2	3.0	5.2	3.2	4.0	6.4	
3491 Metal barrels, drums, and pails	5.0	.4	1.0	.5	3.5	6.2	
3493 Steel springs	4.1	1.4	.7	1.2	2.3	2.3	4.3
3519 Internal combustion engines, n.e.c.	3.3	.3	1.6	.7	3.2	6.1	2.8

SIC Description	1954-58 (1)	1958-63 (2)	1963-66 (3)	1958-65 (4)	1966-69 (5)	1969-70 (6)	1971-73 (7)
3522 Farm machinery and equipment	2.8	1.9	2.1	1.9	3.9	2.2	
3531 Construction machinery	5.0	1.9	2.6	2.1	5.2	5.1	
3532 Mining machinery and equipment	7.5	2.2	1.5	1.7	3.8	3.5	
3535 Conveyors and conveying equipment	6.0	1.6	2.3	1.6	3.1	4.2	
3536 Hoists, cranes, and monorails	5.8	—.5	2.1	.1	3.3	5.7	
3552 Textile machinery	2.6	.9	1.3	1.0	4.4	2.8	
3553 Woodworking machinery	.4	.8	1.0	1.0	3.8	3.0	
3554 Paper industries machinery	2.5						
3555 Printing trades machinery	—.2	2.7	.9	1.7	8.2	2.3	
3561 Pumps and compressors	4.3						
3564 Blowers and fans	6.0						
3567 Industrial furnaces and ovens	3.8	1.7	4.0	2.2	5.9	9.0	
3576 Scales and balances	3.0	2.1	1.6	1.7	4.6	4.3	3.2
3582 Commercial laundry equipment	3.6						
3586 Measuring and dispensing pumps	7.8						
3611 Electrical measuring instruments	3.4						
3621 Motors and generators	3.7	—1.9	—1.7	—2.2	3.7	7.6	
3623 Welding apparatus	6.4	—.8	—1.0	—1.1	2.4	4.9	
3629 Electrical industrial goods, n.e.c.	2.3						
3634 Electrical housewares and fans	.0	—1.3	—1.3	—1.5	1.6	2.2	
3639 Household appliances, n.e.c.	—.8	—2.5	—.3	—2.1	.8	—.6	
3643 Current-carrying wiring devices	1.4						
3651 Radio and television receiving sets	—.2	—2.2	—1.6	—2.0	—2.3	—1.4	
3662 Radio and television communication equipment	2.2						
3674 Semiconductors		.0	—6.1	—2.3	3.8	.1	—.8
3699 Electrical products, n.e.c.	2.3						
3729 Aircraft equipment, n.e.c.	3.9						
3731 Ship building and repairing	1.3						
3811 Engineering and scientific instruments	2.1						
3831 Optical instruments and lenses	4.4						
3841 Surgical and medical instruments	2.3						
3842 Surgical appliances and supplies	3.3						
3843 Dental equipment and supplies	4.6						
3871 Watches and clocks	1.5	.1	—.6	—.4	3.6	1.3	
3911 Jewelry, precious metal		1.1	1.2	1.3	3.1	5.9	
3931 Musical instruments and parts	—.5	1.1	2.4	1.3	3.7	2.5	

Table B-1 (continued)

SIC Description	1954-58 (1)	1958-63 (2)	1963-66 (3)	1958-65 (4)	1966-69 (5)	1969-70 (6)	1971-73 (7)
3943 Children's vehicles	3.2	—.7	1.6	—.2	2.8	6.2	
3949 Sporting and athletic goods, n.e.c.	2.2	1.0	2.2	1.3	1.5	2.5	
3951 Pens and mechanical pencils	—4.1	—.2	1.8	—.1	.2	.0	
3952 Lead pencils and art goods	4.2	.7	.7	.7	2.2	4.6	
3953 Marking devices	—1.2						
3955 Carbon paper and inked ribbons	.0	.1	.8	.2	.0	—1.7	
3963 Buttons	3.4	.2	.7	.3	4.7	8.3	
3964 Needles, pins, and fasteners	.5	—1.3	.5	—.8	1.9	3.8	

Industries with Concentration Ratios Greater than 50 Percent and Less than or Equal to 75 Percent

SIC Description	1954-58 (1)	1958-63 (2)	1963-66 (3)	1958-65 (4)	1966-69 (5)	1969-70 (6)	1971-73 (7)
2032 Canned specialties	1.0	—.8	1.7	—.5	3.7	—.1	
2045 Blended and prepared flour	.3	3.7	1.4	3.2	1.1	.9	
2046 Wet corn milling	—.2	—1.1	3.5	.1	—2.2	8.6	
2052 Cookies, crackers, and biscuits	1.3	.5	1.5	.6	3.0	4.5	4.4
2062 Cane sugar refining	1.8	6.1	—4.6	1.5	3.1	5.4	7.5
2063 Beet sugar	1.4	6.1	—4.5	1.5	2.5	6.2	5.2
2072 Chocolate and cocoa products	—.7	—1.8	1.0	—1.3	9.6	3.0	
2085 Distilled liquors, except brandy	.2	.1	—.5	—.2	.0	3.2	
2087 Flavorings, extracts, and syrups, n.e.c.	.0						
2093 Vegetable oil mills, n.e.c.	—2.4	—1.2	2.8	.9	—.3	11.2	
2095 Roasted coffee	.8	—4.2	4.9	—1.0	4.7	10.8	
2121 Cigars	—.6	.0	.1	.0	1.2	2.8	1.6
2131 Chewing and smoking tobacco	4.7	3.5	4.0	3.2	2.1	7.8	1.8
2141 Tobacco stemming and redrying	2.5						
2231 Weaving and finishing mills, wool	—1.3	.7	2.6	1.3	1.0	1.0	
2271 Woven carpets and rugs	.1	—.4	1.5	.3	—.9	.2	
2234 Thread mills	—1.5	1.6	1.0	1.2	5.5	4.1	
2291 Felt goods, n.e.c.	1.2						
2297 Scouring and combing plants	—3.1	2.8	.3	1.5	—3.0	—12.0	
2646 Pressed and molded pulp goods	.1						
2647 Sanitary paper products		.2	1.2	.2	4.2	7.8	2.4
2654 Sanitary food containers	1.6	.3	—.2	—.2	2.3	2.7	2.0
2655 Fiber cans, drums, and related material	1.5	—.8	.6	—.4	—.3	2.4	
2771 Greeting card manufacturing	2.5						
2812 Alkalies and chlorine	1.6	—.3	1.0	.2	2.0	2.8	
2813 Industrial gases	—1.5	.3	.2	.3	—2.4	9.5	
2816 Inorganic pigments	2.1	.1	2.1	.9	1.2	.0	
2818 Industrial organic chemicals, n.e.c.	—.4	—2.1	—.8	—1.8	—2.1	.1	
2822 Synthetic rubber	—1.5	.4	—1.3	—.3	—.2	.5	.5
2833 Medicinals and botanicals	—4.0	—6.7	—.8	—5.0	—.9	3.0	
2841 Soap and other detergents	.9	—.4	1.1	.2	1.8	.6	

SIC Description	1954-58 (1)	1958-63 (2)	1963-66 (3)	1958-65 (4)	1966-69 (5)	1969-70 (6)	1971-73 (7)
2861 Gum and wood chemicals	3.0						
2892 Explosives	1.4	2.5	—.8	1.7	2.5	2.1	3.0
2895 Carbon black	1.5						
2999 Petroleum and coal products, n.e.c.	5.3						
3011 Tires and inner tubes	3.0	—2.5	1.2	—1.8	2.4	3.6	
3021 Rubber footwear	.3	2.1	1.0	1.8	2.7	6.2	
3121 Industrial leather belting	.8	1.5	2.5	1.3	4.3	5.2	7.9
3221 Glass containers	4.2	—1.1	1.2	—.5	5.4	4.7	2.8
3229 Pressed and blown glass, n.e.c.	1.6	1.7	.6	1.2	5.5	—1.2	
3261 Vitreous plumbing fixtures	.5	—1.8	2.9	—.5	2.4	2.4	4.0
3262 Vitreous china food utensils	5.5	.9	3.1	1.2	7.1	7.6	5.5
3263 Fine earthenware food utensils	6.6	1.6	1.2	1.1	4.2	3.7	7.1
3291 Abrasive products	3.2	.5	—.1	.2	3.5	4.0	
3292 Asbestos products	2.8	1.3	.9	1.2	2.6	4.7	
3296 Mineral wood	—3.7						
3333 Primary zinc	—1.8	3.2	7.0	5.8	.1	4.6	16.2
3339 Primary nonferrous metals, n.e.c.	1.4	2.8	2.4	3.4	9.7	19.0	23.3
3352 Aluminum rolling and drawing	2.9	—1.0	—1.4	—1.0	2.7	3.8	
3411 Metal cans	4.1	.7	1.8	.9	2.9	4.5	5.6
3421 Cutlery	3.4	1.4	1.5	1.1	2.4	7.2	
3496 Collapsible tubes	2.4	.1	—.6	—.1	—.5	10.5	3.6
3497 Metal foil and leaf	6.4						
3534 Elevators and moving stairways	4.4	.2	.7	.4	2.5	9.6	1.0
3537 Industrial trucks and tractors	6.8	2.1	1.4	1.7	4.5	4.4	3.2
3562 Ball and roller bearings	5.1	—2.0	—2.5	—2.5	3.2	.0	2.9
3579 Office machines, n.e.c.	2.4	1.1	3.4	1.7	4.4	4.2	
3581 Automatic merchandising machines	2.4	1.5	1.5	1.3	2.5	5.2	
3612 Transformers	3.1	—3.7	.0	—3.0	1.1	2.4	.6
3613 Switchgear and switch-board apparatus	3.6	—.2	2.7	.8	2.0	5.4	.4
3622 Industrial controls	6.8						
3631 Household cooking equipment	2.0	.0	.2	.0	1.6	4.2	
3632 Household refrigerators and freezers	—2.5	—3.4	—1.7	—2.9	2.7	1.6	
3652 Phonograph records	2.5	1.6	.4	1.3	4.0	.9	3.9
3673 Electron tubes, transmitting	1.5	.0	—5.1	—2.3	1.1	2.2	1.9
3691 Storage batteries	—.6						
3693 X-ray apparatus and tubes	5.6						.5
3694 Engine electrical equipment	1.8	.7	1.9	1.2	6.1	7.0	
3715 Truck trailers	3.2						
3721 Aircraft	4.1						
3722 Aircraft engines and engine parts	3.0						
3742 Railroad and street cars	6.5	1.1	—.1	.6	4.9	5.7	
3751 Motorcycles, bicycles, and parts	—1.5	—1.0	.2	—.9	3.3	2.2	

SIC Description	1954-58 (1)	1958-63 (2)	1963-66 (3)	1958-65 (4)	1966-69 (5)	1969-70 (6)	1971-73 (7)
3822 Automatic temperature controls	6.8						
3851 Ophthalmic goods	—1.1						
3861 Photographic equipment and supplies	2.6	1.2	1.6	1.5	.9	2.4	
3872 Watch cases	2.5						
3914 Silverware and plated ware		3.2	2.3	3.0	11.2	1.1	

Industries with Concentration Ratios Greater than 75 Percent

SIC Description	1954-58 (1)	1958-63 (2)	1963-66 (3)	1958-65 (4)	1966-69 (5)	1969-70 (6)	1971-73 (7)
2043 Cereal preparations	2.4	1.9	4.2	2.3	4.1	4.6	
2073 Chewing gum	4.3	1.8	—1.0	.9	.0	7.0	1.1
2111 Cigarettes	1.2	.6	1.5	.6	3.8	6.9	2.3
2296 Tire cord and fabric	—2.1	—1.3	.2	—.9	.1	.0	
2823 Cellulose manmade fibers	—1.1	—1.1	.8	—.5	.6	—.1	3.2
2824 Organic fibers, noncellulosic	—5.6	—1.6	—3.2	—2.3	—2.9	—1.1	—.1
3031 Reclaimed rubber	.0	.0	.0	.0	.0		
3211 Flat glass	2.3	—1.2	—.4	—1.0	4.7	5.7	
3275 Gypsum products	3.1	.9	—.9	.4	1.2	—3.3	6.5
3313 Electrometallurgical products	6.8	—5.7	—2.0	—4.6	—1.0	17.4	
3331 Primary copper	—2.3	3.6	5.5	5.0	10.6	21.8	
3334 Primary aluminum							.0
3392 Nonferrous forgings	1.5						
3511 Steam engines and turbines	2.5	—2.0	1.7	—1.2	5.6	9.3	
3572 Typewriters	3.3	.5	.5	.5	.9	2.2	1.4
3624 Carbon and graphite products	6.6	.0	1.2	.2	—.4	4.4	2.8
3633 Household laundry equipment	.8	—1.2	—.8	—1.2	1.8	2.2	
3635 Household vacuum cleaners	—1.0	—2.6	—2.5	—2.3	—.9	.0	.1
3641 Electric lamps	2.7	2.8	—.2	1.9	.3	4.5	2.9
3661 Telephone and telegraph apparatus	—3.1						
3671 Electron tubes, receiving type	3.2	.0	—.4	—.8	8.4	9.0	4.6
3672 Cathode ray picture tubes	—2.1	—.1	—12.4	—4.9	—4.1	—2.2	—1.3
3692 Primary batteries, dry and wet	6.1	—.9	.9	—.5	5.8	1.9	2.1
3717 Motor vehicles and parts	4.1	.1	.8	.3	1.7	3.7	
3741 Locomotives and parts	2.5	.1	.3	.2	.5	2.6	

a n.e.c. = not elsewhere classified.

Source: Column (1): U.S. Bureau of the Census, *Census of Manufactures, 1963*, vol. 4, "Census Unit Value Indexes." Columns (2) — (6): U.S. Bureau of Labor Statistics, Wholesale Price Index, compiled for four-digit SIC industries by U.S. Department of Commerce, Bureau of Economic Analysis, and Federal Reserve Board. Column (7): U.S. Bureau of Labor Statistics, Industry Sector Price Indexes. Data for some industries were available only for 1954-58 or 1958-70.